Qualicum Beach Memorial Golf Club Men's Amateur Tournament: 1991 Darren Griff Nanaimo 1992 Ron MacDonald Nanaimo 1993 Darren Griff Nanaimo 1994 Darrren Griff Nanaimo 1995 Sandy Harper Nanaimo 1996 Steve Watson Vancouver 1997 Bruce Harper Nanaimo 1998 Ryner Wilson Fairwinds 1999 Jordan Caron Morningstar 2000 Jordan Caron Morningstar 2001 Steve Berry Arbutus Ridge 2002 Craig Keeping BCGA Players' Club 2003 Brodie Williams Nanaimo 2004 Steve Berry BCGA Players' Club 2005 Matt Cella Nanaimo 2006 Sandy Harper Nanaimo 2007 Mark Kitts Morningstar 2008 Sandy Harper Nanaimo 2009 Sandy Harper Nanaimo 2010 Steve Watson BCGA Players' Club 2011 Sandy Harper Nanaimo **Qualicum Beach Memorial Golf Club Ladies 18 Hole Club Championship:** 1955 Ruby Crowley 1956 Ruby Crowley 1957 Jeanette Forrester 1958 Jeanette Forrester 1959 Jeanette Forrester 1961 Helen Eve 1962 Jeanette Forrester 1963 Jeanette Forrester 1964 Jeanette Forrester 1965 Jeanette Forrester 1966 Jeanette Forrester 1967 Jeanette Forrester 1968 Jeanette Forrester 1970 Helen Eve 1971 Helen Eve 1972 Maureen Bridge 1973 Eve Johnson 1974 Maureen Bridge 1975 Maureen Bridge 1976 Maureen Bridge 1977 Maureen Bridge 1978 Joy Boyes 1979 Joy Boyes 1980 Joy Boyes 1981 Joy Boyes 1982 Maureen Bridge 1983 Joan Prendergast 1984 Corrine Floyd 1985 Bev Lasure 1986 Margaret Thompson 1987 Joan Prendergast 1988 Margaret Thompson 1989 Margaret Thompson 1990 Margaret Thompson 1991 Bev Lasure 1992 Margaret Thompson 1993 Margaret Thompson 1994 Margaret Thompson 1995 Margaret Thompson 1996 Margaret Thompson 1997 Bev Lasure 1998 Margaret Thompson 1999 Shirley Elliott 2000 Mikey Aylesworth 2001 Mikey Aylesworth 2002 Mikey Aylesworth 2003 Mikey Aylesworth 2004 Mikey Aylesworth 2005 Mikey Aylesworth 2006 Edie Gross 2007 Lynn Gordon 2008 Barb Chapman 2009 Susan Paterson 2010 Susan Paterson 2011 Susan Paterson **Qualicum Beach Memorial Golf Club Men's Championship For the Nigel Bourke Trophy:** 1948 F.O. White 1949 J. Egger 1951 J. Egger 1952 R. Forrester 1953 H.K. Reid 1954 J. Prowse 1955 R. Forrester 1956 Peter Barr 1957 Peter Barr 1958 H.K. Reid 1959 H.K. Reid 1960 Peter Barr 1961 Peter Barr 1962 Peter Barr 1963 Jerry Gisleus 1964 Peter Barr 1965 Peter Barr 1967 Neil Higgs 1968 Al Norris 1969 Pitt Clayton 1971 Art Bridge 1972 Art Bridge 1973 Art Bridge 1974 Art Bridge 1975 R. Logan 1976 R. Logan 1977 R. Logan 1978 D. McCullough 1979 Art Bridge 1980 B. MacDonald 1981 R. Kennedy 1982 Art Bridge 1983 K. Floyd 1984 –Jack Parker 1985 Pat Collins 1986 Jack Parker 1987 Jack Parker 1988 William Crowther 1989 Jim Wilson 1990 William Crowther 1991 Ralph Baddeley 1992 Ralph Baddeley 1993 Jack Parker 1994 Ted Powell 1995 Ted Powell 1996 Jack Parker 1997 Ajit Manhas 1998 Brook Castelsky 1999 Bryan Phelan 2000 Ernie Bentley 2001 Burke Bullock 2002 Ernie Bentley 2003 Ray Deptuck 2004 Bill Bennett 2005 Bill Bennett

2006 Mike Hansen 2007 Mike Hansen 2008 Peter Drummond 2009 Mike Hansen 2010 Mike Hansen 2011 Les Pockett **Qualicum Beach Memorial Golf Club Ladies' 9 Hole Championship:** 1984 Rene Hilton 1985 Rene Hilton 1986 Val Monroe 1987 Olive Buchanan 1988 Evelyn Swinburne 1989 Eva Philpott 1990 Eva Philpott 1991 Olive Buchanan 1992 Iris Page 1993 Daphne Norman 1994 Brenda MacFie 1995 Gerry Philippe 1996 Iris Page 1997 Win Trusdale 1998 Jean Powell 1999 Iris Page 2000 Gladys Morton 2001 Martha Sundquist 2002 Martha Sundquist 2003 Adele Yeomans 2004 Joan Forgie 2005 Joan Forgie 2006 Joan Forgie 2007 Sheila Humphreys 2008 Pat Rooke 2009 Joan Forgie 2010 Sheila Humphreys 2011 Pat Rooke **Qualicum Beach Memorial Golf Club Presidents:** 1981-1982 Arthur Bridge 1982-1983 Drake McRae 1983-1984 Hank Bennett 1984-1985 John Watson 1985-1986 Jay Wood 1986-1987 Jim Turner 1987-1988 Jim Turner 1988-1989 Joy Barber 1989-1990 Bob Tait 1990-1991 Harry Ronmark 1991-1992 Bill Stevens 1992-1993 Bob Tait 1993-1994 Harvey Robinson 1994-1995 Howard Perrigo 1995-1996 Rob Hughes 1996-1997 Shirley Elliott 1997-1998 Shirley Elliott 1998-1999 Tats Aoki 1999-2000 Bill Fayter 2000-2001 Bob Wade 2001-2002 Ray Zoost 2002-2003 Ken Vail 2003-2004 Pat Chern 2004-2005 Roy Cope 2005-2006 Terry L'Ami 2006-2007 Len Lloyd 2007-2008 George Mooney 2008-2009 John Lajoie 2009-2010 Don Reid 2010-1011 Tony Sharp 2011-2012 Doug Ebbett **Qualicum Beach Memorial Golf Club Adam and Eve Trophy:** 1986 Iris Page Ray Elder 1987 Gloria Miller Bert Mallinger 1988 Bev Reber Bill Fayter 1989 Helen Williams Bob Tait 1990 Ann Kehoe Dick Garrett 1991 Mary Varney Jim Thompson 1992 Shirley Elliott Cliff Brodie 1993 Carmen Bondue Stan Roy 1994 Kate Mitchell Bob Trusdale 1995 Verna Bennett Dave Watson 1996 Eileen Dobson Ajit Manhas 1997 Gerry Phillippe Bryan Kanarens 1998 Adele Yeomans George Ashcroft 1999 Pat Clover Ted Mangnall 2000 Kay McIntyre Dave Watson 2001 Eleanor Geddes Lyall Sundberg 2002 Eleanor Geddes Ken Vail 2004 Ann Lajoie Charles MacIntyre 2005 Jean Ashcroft Jim Reynolds 2006 Ev Dimond Jim Reynolds 2007 Pat & John Rooke 2008 Gerry & Ken Calthorpe 2009 Tom & Helan Waller 2010 Lyn Bailey Alex Briden 2011 Rod & Carol Sharpe **Qualicum Beach Memorial Golf Club Ladies 9 Hole Eclectic Low Gross:** 1983 Val Monro 1984 Tenna Johnson 1985 Rene' Hilton 1986 Iris Page 1987 Val Monro 1988 Eve Hilborn 1989 Mary Leece 1990 Eva Philpott 1991 Iris Page & Gerry Phillippe 1992-1993 Iris Page 1994-1995 Brenda MacFie 1996 Ann Panton & Yvette Edgar 1997 Gerry Phillippe 1998 Jean Bates & Pauline Kneale & Iris Page & Jean Powell 1999 Iris Page 2000 Pat Rooke 2001 Marge Rathwell 2002 Iris Page & Pat Rooke 2003 Joan Forgie 2004 Hilary Avis 2005 Iris Page 2006-2007-2008 Sheila Humphreys 2009 Pat Rooke & Nicky Gardner & Sheila Humphreys 2010 Sheila Humphreys 2011 Joan Forgie

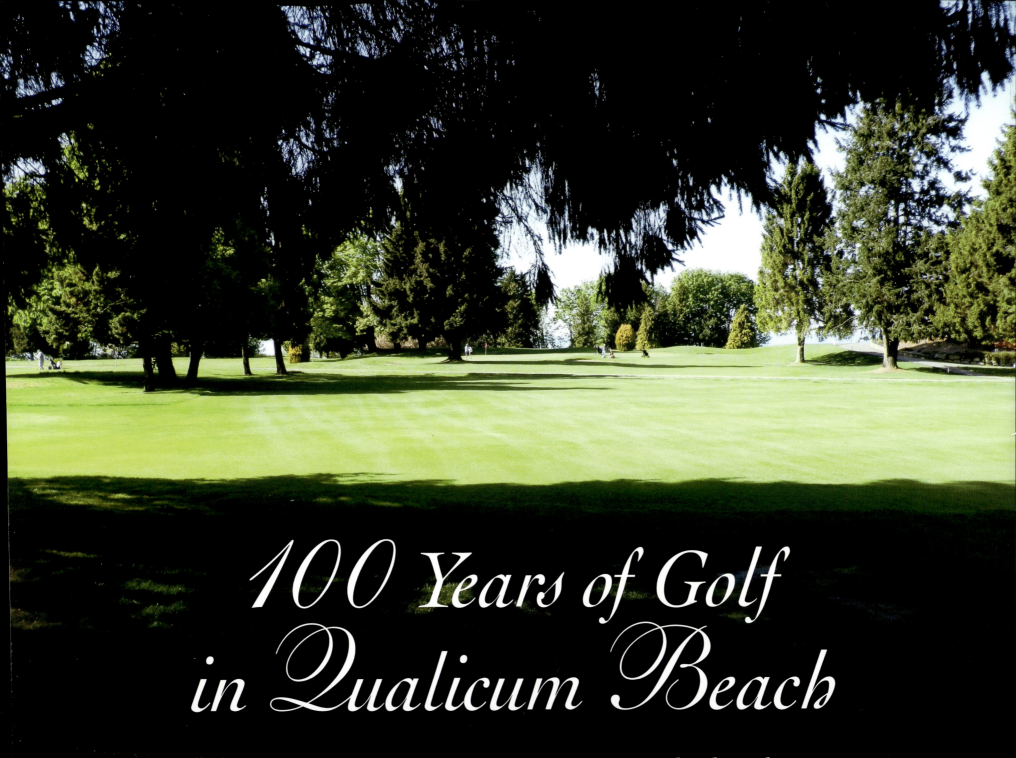

100 Years of Golf in Qualicum Beach

Claud Buchanan

Photograph by Lois L. Brown Photography.

Library and Archives Canada Cataloguing in Publication

Buchanan, Claud N.

100 years of golf in Qualicum Beach / Claud N. Buchanan.

Includes bibliographical references.

ISBN 978-0-9879525-0-9

1. Qualicum Beach Memorial Golf Course (Qualicum Beach, B.C.)--History. I. Title. II. Title: One hundred years of golf in Qualicum Beach.

GV969.Q35B83 2012   796.352'0607112   C2012-903000-7

2012 by Claud Buchanan. All rights reserved.

Printed in Canada.

Introduction
page 07

The Beginning
page 15

The Formative Years
page 25

Personalities
page 45

The Playing Professionals
page 77

The Present
page 85

FOREWORD

Golf in Qualicum Beach goes back a long way in my family – my father claimed to have sneaked onto the course as a 12 year-old in 1921. I learned to play golf in Qualicum Beach, first with an old hickory-shafted rusty 7 iron on the sand at low tide. As I got older and more proficient, it would be a great occasion to be invited to play a round with adults, where we would be strictly taught the fine points of golf etiquette. And with no irrigation on the fairways until the mid 1960s, it was not uncommon to hit 300-yard drives, particularly on the present seventh hole as a well-hit ball rolled seemingly forever over the dry grass.

The course, designed by Arthur Vernon Macan, was built in 1913 as part of the attraction for The Qualicum Beach Hotel. The hotel, demolished in 1972, was located on the entire block opposite the current third fairway.

Golf, along with a beautiful beach and renowned salmon fishing, made the hotel into what today would be called a preferred destination resort. This combination of golf and fishing once attracted Hollywood celebrities to our area every summer – the likes of Bob Hope and Bing Crosby would anchor their yachts off the Shady Rest and the Shell Station, and spend several weeks enjoying golf and fishing. These celebrities could afford to vacation anywhere in the world, but the fact that they came here is indicative of the appeal the golf course in Qualicum Beach had to offer, as it was one of the few places on the west coast of the U.S. or Canada where you could play golf and stay at sea on your yacht. Perhaps another appeal was the fact that in Qualicum Beach they were out of the glare of publicity.

In recent years, other courses built in the area have provided different golf experiences, but Qualicum Beach Memorial Golf Course remains a unique 9-hole layout so popular that it is fully subscribed by the club members, with a waiting list.

This book documents the long history of the course's place in the community and the people who have contributed to its development in various capacities. I hope you'll enjoy this history of the first 100 years.

Jack Wilson
Town Councillor & golfer
September 2011

Introduction

INTRODUCTION

Qualicum Beach, a community nestled so comfortably by Mother Nature into the mid-east coast of Vancouver Island, is an unforgettable scenic gem. When approaching from the south, the full sweep of Qualicum Bay with its several miles of unspoiled white sands greets the visitor passing by the end of Judges Row, a collection of mansion-like homes that tell of an era when Qualicum Beach was the 'Victoria' of the mid-island.

Its golf course, a sea-girt nine holes of beautifully manicured fairways and lush rolling greens, appears to the immediate left of the highway, and its sudden appearance opposite Judges Row is almost enough to distract the unwary driver who sees it for the first time. Such is the onset of its verdant beauty.

Because the golf course consists of nine holes only, the membership quota (about four hundred) is invariably full and the waiting list is often quite lengthy. However, because of this, the retirement nature of golf becomes a factor and the membership and green fees are generally lower than the longer local courses. Golf in Qualicum Beach is affordable for many retirees. The club is a non-profit organization.

The panoramic view across the Strait of Georgia from the recently completed clubhouse (February 2008) is one of encompassing beauty. Prominent in the background to the east is the British Columbia mainland fronted by Lasqueti and Texada Islands, while to the north the profiles of Hornby and Denman Islands are easily recognizable.

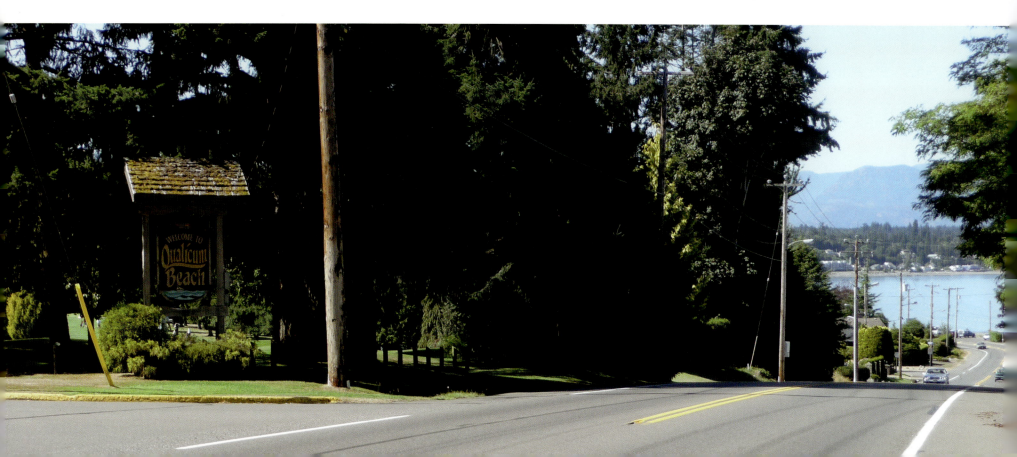

Those who take the time to look will see a little group of rocky islands called "The Sisters," eight miles out into the Strait directly facing the golf course. This little nest of rather barren rocks is home to one of the destaffed lighthouses – The Sisters Islets Light – on the Pacific Coast of British Columbia.

During May and June of each year, the course is adorned by the blossoms of an amazing variety of trees – chestnut, plum, apple, cherry, pear and dogwood are some of the better known varieties. Along some of the fairways are luscious blackberry bushes that attract a great many honeybees.

Eagles are not the only birds that make this golf course their home. The meadowlark often raises its melodic song to accompany the resident deer quietly meandering among the bushes that guard the creek where they raise their families. Ducks – often Mergansers – geese, heron, and pheasant all live happily here. The occasional bear has been seen and rare sightings of cougar also occur.

Beach Creek, which flows through the course, is home to beaver and muskrat. The creek housed a trout hatchery, tended by Art Higgs, some time ago and salmon and trout still occasionally spawn in its sheltered waters. In season, sea lions lounging on the offshore rocks give vent to their raucous unmelodic bellowing and when the wind blows in from the ocean they can be heard a long way off.

From the first tee there is Mount Arrowsmith with its near-eternal snows smiling, and sometimes, on a wet day, glowering down on us the most fortunate golfers, certainly in this part of the world. And the eagle tree – a giant fir – hard by the ocean just past the first green, is a treasured feature of many local photographs. Often on a fine day these majestic birds perch at the top of the rather rickety branches, alert for what might serve as an unwary meal either in the bushes or the shallow ocean. Below the eagle tree, stretching literally for miles are warm, wide, sun-drenched sandy beaches; safe beaches for families since they are shallow and the waters warm and caressing.

The signature hole is the fifth, called the 'Gulley', a short par three where the player is confronted by a very deep ravine at the bottom of which is a little creek – Beach Creek.

Standing on the seventh tee, look to the right and Elizabeth Avenue, which we are told was once quite a substantial part of the golf course, stretches parallel to the fairway for all its length. On the left, the white mansion that once was R.A. Brown's home is still to the fore. Towering behind all of this is Mount Arrowsmith from which the Coast Range of mountains extends.

The golfer could be forgiven for simply standing there and drinking in the vista that unfolds over all of what this God-given links has to offer and gently gives reminders of those who have gone before, treading these hallowed fairways creating historic footprints for those still to follow. Few communities are blessed with such a golf facility set in their midst, and with such gorgeous natural beauty surrounding all of this unique setting.

The terrain, on which the golf course was built, was originally quite thickly wooded. Very tall pine, fir, cedar, alder, some birch and lesser numbers of incidental trees covered the countryside that would become the golf course.

No heavy machinery was available for the work and all equipment was delivered from Nanaimo by horse. First Nation and Chinese crews cleared and levelled the land by hand. This was the Qualicum Golf Course now known as the Qualicum Beach Memorial Golf Club, and its construction, along with the building of the Qualicum Beach Inn, was done under the impetus of General Noel Money and the guiding hand of course designer Arthur Macan.

The original layout stretched from what is now Elm Street on the west to the corner of Crescent Road East and highway 19A on the east. There was also a triangle of the course on the waterside of the highway where Judges Row begins now. As can be seen from Jack Parker's diagrams, (see page 65) players were required to shoot over Memorial Avenue on two holes. Memorial was little more than a cart track at that time.

The course opened in 1913 with Ted Havemeyer, a golfer from Jerico Club, Vancouver, as its first President. Ted inaugurated the Upper Island Amateur Championship, which quickly became a popular May 24th weekend tournament attracting B.C.'s top golfers.

At the outbreak of the First World War and the conversion of the Qualicum Beach Hotel to a convalescent hospital, the golf course was closed for four years. Sheep belonging to a local resident, Captain Matheson, grazed contentedly on the fairways. Gas-powered tractors did not appear until 1912 at Shaughnessy Heights in Vancouver which was why, prior to 1915, the game was a winter pastime and not year-round. The season began in September and ended in June because the courses had no method for cutting the grass to a playable length during the growing season. The four-footed friends – sheep, goats and cattle – could not trim the grass to an appropriate length.

The first greens Superintendents at Qualicum Beach were probably Neddie Kennedy who, in turn was followed by Frank Topliffe of Qualicum Beach. One season in the early thirties, General Money could not pay Topliffe and in lieu of wages gave him three building lots. Topliffe's brother, ten year-old Bert, was hired by General Noel Money to weed the greens. Bert, a resident of

Eagle Tree at 1st Green.

Coombs and now ninety-four years of age, remembers using a weeding tool that resembled a bent screwdriver for weeding and gasoline for killing the roots. The greens Topliffe weeded were quite small and watered by a type of self-propelled sprinkler that had to be turned on individually every evening since no proper watering system would be installed until the 1960s.

In 1940, a company formed by Leonard Boultbee, F.O. White and Fred Sweet purchased the Inn and golf links from General Money for $50,000. Five years later, the golf club obtained the services of Ernie Tate and later Dave MacLeod, one of the leading professional golfers and teachers in the province. J.A. Montgomerie took over in the pro shop after MacLeod's death. R.A. Brown and associates from Calgary bought the layout in 1954.

Alex Smith acted as manager and erstwhile professional from 1958 until 1981, with the assistance of Jon Leyne and Peter Olynyk, both professional golfers. Steve Cikaluk succeeded Olynyk in 1981, the year the golf course was purchased by the town. He, in turn, was followed by Ross Mantell in March of 2004. He is the current professional.

The partnership between the town and golf club which began in 1981 has continued to flourish over the last thirty years. As the centennial approaches in 2013, it is hoped that this symbiotic relationship will foster even greater goodwill and warmth.

The present-day Crescent Road in 1913. General Money's white house, later "Bobby" Brown's, can clearly be seen in the centre background. The shed in the foreground is roughly where the present day (2011) third tee box is located. The photographer would have been standing where Beach Road meets the Crescent.

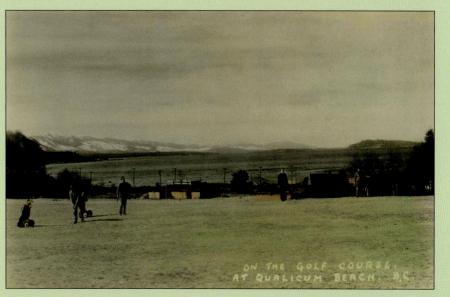

The Golfer's Prayer

Dear lord, when I depart this life,
And enter heaven's gate,
I hope you'll have a golf course there,
With reasonable rates.
With fairways that are carpet like,
All soft and green and cheery,
Greens that run true to the hole,
And gullies somewhat scary.

I hope you'll have some cherry trees
That bloom so bright each spring,
Great cedars, firs and chestnuts,
Fruit trees and everything.
If you could have some little fawns
That gambol on the green.
While mama watches proudly,
Oh lord, that would be keen.

If the fairways stretched along the beach
Of some blue rippled sea,
Where I could see the mountains
As I stand upon the tee.
If I could gaze into the sky,
And see great eagles soar,
Dear lord, could mortals such as I,
Dare ask for any more.

If it could have great flocks of geese,
And sea lions in the spring,
Raucous crows and sea gulls,
And pretty birds that sing.
If I could stand upon the tee,
And looking far and wide,
See nothing but the beauty,
Of a peaceful countryside.

These things, dear lord, I humbly ask,
When I pass through the Gates.
As well as camaraderie
With all my golfing mates.
Then lord I had a second thought,
For now, I need not come,
'Cause all those things await me,
On the links at Qualicum.

©2002 Gus Barrett

The Beginning

A 1911 photo taken at the junction of what is now Memorial Avenue and Crescent Road, before the golf course existed, looking south. Imagine then, what the clearing of the woodland must have been like. No equipment comparable to what exists today was available. The trees were cut down and the roots either dynamited or forcibly removed by teams of oxen and horses using large grappling hooks. The holes that remained had to be filled in. For a number of years the fairways were very rough and rocky. Golf clubs were easily damaged. Not much clearing or watering of the fairways was done until the 1950s. The greens were very small and bunkers did not exist.

PHOTO BY THE R.C.A.F.　　AN AIR VIEW OF THE QUALICUM BEACH HOTEL AND GOLF COURSE,　Vancouver Island Series No. 3
VANCOUVER ISLAND, B.C.

A very early photo of the Qualicum Beach Hotel. The Crescent Road runs parallel to the bottom of the photo and the little red-roofed building was the Caddy Shack, the very first 'clubhouse' of the golf club. The two new blue-roofed wings of the hotel were built to house important visitors. The street running uphill to the right of the hotel is Beach Road and the new railway station (1914) can be seen at the top. The tee box for the first fairway is in front of the Caddy Shack and there is a path leading directly from the hotel across the first fairway down to the beach.

The house with the red roof in the bottom right of the photo is the Dill residence and was built by the hotel builders for a place to stay during the construction. Note that the original clubhouse proper has not yet been built in front of the hotel. The hotel was not open all year round since no insulation was used in its structure. Likewise, the golf course saw only limited play since no equipment was available to keep the grass mown to an acceptable level. Sheep were actually the first 'mowers'.

THE BEGINNING | 17

Arthur Vernon Macan | 1882 – 1964

Through the Mists of Time

By the early 1900s, the winds of World War I had begun to blow across Europe. Peace, however, still reigned in North America and a 20 year-old American, amateur golfer Francis Ouimet with his 10 year-old caddie, Eddie Lowery, defeated the British professionals Harry Vardon and Ted Ray in a playoff to win the US Open Championship at Brookline, Massachusetts, on September 20, 1913.

Vernon Macan

Far away across the Atlantic Ocean, a young Irish lawyer, Arthur Vernon Macan living in a prestigious area of Dublin, for no apparent reason at the time, abruptly uprooted his family and moved to Victoria, British Columbia. At this stage in his life he was already one of the top five amateur golfers in his native Ireland.

Macan had trained as a lawyer at Trinity College, met and married Juliet Richards, daughter of a prominent member of the local judiciary. Macan seemed to be headed for a successful career in Law. As it turned out he had no heart for the legal profession and chose to pursue his dream as a golfer by moving to Victoria in the spring of 1910 where he found employment with the Government Division of Lands and Forests.

Macan joined the Victoria Golf Club and won the BC Men's Amateur Championship in 1912. By 1913, he had won the PNGA (Pacific National Golf Association) Men's title. Also in that year, a flurry of land purchases had been taking place at an obscure but beautiful little place called Qualicum Beach whose only claim to fame was its physical allure – spectacular ocean views, miles of virgin beaches, lush green forests and one or two cascading rivers.

1,300 acres of this gorgeous seascape had been purchased by the Merchants Trust and Trading Company of Newcastle, England, at the urging of Canadian-born General Noel Money who saw Qualicum Beach as a summer retreat for Victoria residents and as many upper class individuals as he could persuade to invest in his project.

General Money was a born promoter and soon his vision of a splendid resort hotel and golf course to match was about to come to fruition. The fact that Money and Macan were both members of the Victoria Golf Club was conducive to Macan's offering to lay out the General's golf course for him. Which Macan did. (There is no record of his fee for the work.)

The hotel and golf course (not the golf club) were completed at roughly the same time – 1913. The golf course supposedly was intended to accommodate eighteen holes. The railway and its station building came one year later.

At the outbreak of war in that same year Macan joined the Canadian Overseas Expeditionary Force, 88th Victoria Fusiliers. He and his company embarked for overseas service on May 23rd, 1916, Macan's birthday. In England he was trained to operate the relatively new Lewis Gun, not knowing he was destined to do battle at Vimy Ridge in Northern France.

Sometime between the setting of the sun on Easter Sunday and the call to battle April 9, 1917, a shell exploded next to Vernon Macan's foot. The explosion destroyed his left heel and gangrene quickly set into the wound. In order to save his entire leg it was amputated six inches below his knee.

He elected to spend time recuperating at the family home at 53 Merion Square, Dublin, after which Macan returned to Victoria. His wife, son Arthur Jr. and daughter Juliet arrived soon after and took up residence at 1123 Newport Avenue. Their stay was short, and some time between 1922 and 1924 Macan's wife and young family left for Ireland and did not return to Victoria.

By 1921, the course Macan had laid out for General Money at Qualicum Beach in 1913 was in need of renovation and Macan was recalled to oversee the work. As a result the Parksville/Qualicum Beach PROGRESS reported that: "The fairways and greens were in excellent condition, the recent alterations to the course by Vernon Macan being a great improvement."

Macan eventually became the busiest of all golf architects in the Pacific Northwest and California. His business progressed and prospered almost entirely by osmosis.

By 1960 Macan is back in Qualicum Beach again working with Alex Smith, the course greens keeper and manager. Between September 1960 and August 1961 he provided Smith with three detailed reports for improvements to the layout. Finally Macan writes, somewhat frustrated:

"You advised me some time ago you had planned to start construction work in October. I conclude you wish to keep the course open for your summer and early fall play. I have some commitments and would like to know if your plans to start work in October are still in force. I would appreciate if you would forward the $250 balance you promised."

Alex Smith closed the golf course from fall 1967 until fall 1968 to conduct the renovations recommended in Macan's reports. Smith hired Dale Fabrick, a local man, to carry out the renovations required.

In all, Macan designed or reconfigured 55 golf courses in B.C., Washington State and California during his lifetime. And yet he seems little known to many golfers of the present time.

A list of the BC Golf Courses designed or renovated by Macan includes (alphabetically):

- Capilano Golf and Country Club – 1950 R. 1960 R.
- Columbia-Edgewater Golf Club – 1924
- Cowichan Golf Club – 1921
- Fraserview Golf Course R. – 1958
- Gleneagles Golf Course – 1927
- Gorge Vale Golf Club – 1927
- Harrison Golf Course – 1960 R.
- Langara Golf Course – 1924
- Marine Drive Golf Club – 1922, 1924 R. 1947 R. 1962 R.
- McLeery Golf Course – 1956
- Musqueam Golf Course – 1961
- Nanaimo Golf Club – 1953
- Qualicum Beach Golf Club – 1913, 1920 R. 1961 R.
- Royal Colwood Golf and Country Club
  (Royal Colwood Golf Club, Colwood Golf and Country Club) – 1913, 1922 R. 1927 R.
- Shaughnessy Golf and Country Club
  (Shaughnessy Heights Golf and Country Club) – 1926 R. 1957
- University Golf Course – 1928
- Vancouver Golf Club (Vancouver Golf and Country Club) – 1920 R.
- Victoria Golf Club – 1923 R. 11955 R.

Macan died at age 82 while designing the golf course at Sequim, Washington in 1964.

An updated photo – The driveway no longer exists but the surrounding trees are indicative of the kind of vegetation that had to be cleared during the construction of the golf course. Note the canvas golf bag, which was quite typical of the era. The standard garb was plus fours.

General Noel Money is the central figure in this photo.

THE BEGINNING | 21

Nine Or Eighteen Holes?

The perennial debate that has swirled around the links at Qualicum Beach, is the one to determine the number of greens originally built. In other words; was the course nine or eighteen holes on opening day in 1913?

The CPGA golf magazine of 1947 reads:

"The Qualicum Golf Links at Qualicum Beach, Vancouver Island, were built in 1913 and were formally opened for play in 1914 as an 18-hole links." Later in the article, these words;

"Shortly after the outbreak of hostilities in World War 1, the adjacent hotel premises were taken over as a Military Hospital. Consequently while the links were improved from time to time, they were not in active use until 1919 when the Qualicum Golf Club was formed under the direction of General Noel Money.

At this time it was decided to reduce the size of the links to nine holes, and this was accomplished during the year and from then on has been a nine-hole Golf Links."

The Golf Course, therefore, opened in 1914; the Golf Club, under the guidance of General Money, opened in 1919 – one year after the end of World War 1.

Among locals who remember the early days of its operation, there is no unanimity. A post card of 1919 certainly shows the elements of 18 holes, which stretch all the way from the 'Qualicum Seaside Hotel' down to the ocean. Roger Whitmee Jr, born in Qualicum Beach almost eighty years ago remembers that his grandfather spoke of a green and possibly a tee box in the area of present-day Bay Street and Poplar Avenue. He also has memories of a fence that completely surrounded the golf course, which had a very limited season in its initial stages. The main reason for the building of this fence was to keep out cows, which seemed to have access to just about anywhere in the village. Stiles were built at regular intervals for human use. Legend has it that the cows were owned by Gil Mant.

Fran Dobbinson talks about her youth when she lived in a house at the end of Poplar Avenue and is certain that the course extended that far west – about one kilometre from where the present first fairway and green ends; plenty of room for more fairway and greens.

Evelyn and Earle Mitchell say the same. Others differ and it is not the intention of this brief history to say who might be right and who might not. One fact seems to be indisputable; more than nine holes were built by the time Opening Day came along, presumably in May of 1913.

Opening Day was celebrated by staging a tournament on May 24th and closing took place right after Labour Day. The brand new Qualicum Beach Hotel, financed and built by a group called The Merchants' Trust and Trading Company, put together by Harry Beasely, was quickly the focal part of the little town, as was the golf course. It is significant that the railway arrived in 1913 and the station building was completed one year later in 1914.

It is also worth noting that uptown Qualicum Beach barely existed at this time. Memorial Avenue was still a cart track with deep high woods on either side (see photo on page 16).

At best, during the early days, the golf season lasted four months and coincided with the opening and closing of the Qualicum Beach Hotel. Few locals played golf, mostly because the facility was intended for the use of hotel guests – friends and acquaintances of Brigadier General Money. He, too, played golf but wintered at the Empress

Hotel in Victoria. Understandably, neither the hotel nor the golf course made any great profit in their operations. It is worth remembering too that the local population at the time of the golf course opening was just a few hundred souls.

The chief occupation for men at that time was in the three local sawmills. Qualicum Beach was not a retirement centre at this stage in its history and sawmill workers had neither the time nor money to play golf. This would explain why the course was 'mowed' by the grazing of sheep on its fairways.

Bob Bagnall, born in Qualicum Beach in 1925, remembers that only two or three pairs of Canada Geese visited the golf course annually and bred on the fairways. Most fairways were bordered by thick Scotch broom, one of the worst enemies of golfers. A ball hit into the broom was rarely playable. Bagnall who caddied here as a boy tells that local lads had difficulty finding employment since caddies were often 'imported' from Victoria for tournaments. Sometimes this meant carrying two bags instead of one. At age ten, Bagnall was considered too young for carrying a golf bag. He and his local buddies were greatly annoyed at this policy.

By 1935 when he was caddying regularly for Mr. Bob Filberg from Comox, Bagnall states categorically that the course was nine holes only. Fred, Jack and Bert Parker's mother Anne, played the course most of her life after age 40 and never spoke of eighteen holes.

While the controversy will never be brought to a mutually satisfactory conclusion it is perhaps fair to say that the intention to build eighteen holes was always there. Certainly it is clear that more than nine holes were built and plans exist showing the possible layout of an eighteen-hole course. It is acknowledged that, in the early clearing of what is now the golf course, 80 acres were logged and some tree stumps blasted by dynamite; others were removed by teams of horses using a type of hook to extract the remaining roots.

The present-day layout covers 60 acres, leaving a substantial amount of ground (20 acres) that was eventually sold to private individuals and developers.

The outbreak of World War I almost certainly derailed the actual construction. It is worth remembering, too, that the hotel and the course, as it then was, were closed for a minimum of four years during that period. The facility did not reopen until the early 1920s. The only lawn mowers that had serviced the fairways were local farmers' sheep.

By that time and into the 1940s and 50s house lots were sold in the areas of Crescent Road, Poplar Avenue, Bay Street, Elm Avenue and Elizabeth Street plus the west side of Memorial Avenue south of the Island Highway. There was no longer sufficient space for an eighteen hole golf course. In hindsight, this was perhaps a blessing since the cost of maintaining such a facility in a community still in the initial stages of development might have been prohibitive.

The Formative Years

Our Club Houses | 1920 – 2008

Through the Years

The first so-called clubhouse was affectionately called the 'CADDY SHACK' and it had pride of place on what is now the third tee box. The Caddy Shack was a sort of satellite of the Qualicum Beach Resort Hotel, which, along with its outbuildings, swimming pool and tennis courts stood for more than 50 years in roughly the area between Beach Road and Memorial Avenue.

Soon after the hotel was in full operation – basically summer and fall, since there was no insulation in the building – a full-sized, quite elegant clubhouse was constructed on the hotel grounds just off Crescent Road. That building remained as long as the hotel. Both were demolished in 1972, although the hotel actually closed in 1968. Its last owner was Arthur Brown.

Pat Gadd Construction built a new clubhouse in 1970 at the corner of Crescent Road and Memorial Avenue. It served the members for more than 30 years and was added to several times during that period. A major addition was a wraparound patio, which meant that members could eat and entertain outside.

The new long-awaited state-of-the-art clubhouse opened in 2008 and has been a focal point for social gatherings ever since. It houses a restaurant with a large patio from which the ocean views are superb.

This is the only surviving photo of the Caddy Shack that I have been able to find thus far. The gentleman in the photo is Jim Montgomerie, one of the playing professionals at Qualicum Beach. Note the sign on the building indicating a path to the beach. The Caddy Shack served the golfers well until the clubhouse was built on the hotel property. Today the shack is part of the Scout Hall on First Avenue adjacent to the ballpark.

Hotel Clubhouse – This quite elegant building stood in the hotel grounds just across from the Caddy Shack. For a long time it hosted social gatherings, had a full-sized dance floor and bar. The fireplace chimney clearly shows in the photo. It closed in 1968 and was torn down in 1972 when the hotel was demolished. To this day there are regrets that the buildings are no longer there.

Qualicum Beach Memorial Golf Course Club House 1970 – this building stood at the corner of Memorial and The Crescent for more than 30 years. Many changes were made to the original building including new wings that housed the locker rooms and office space. A major addition was a wraparound patio for outdoor dining. The building was demolished in 2009.

The state-of-the-art Club House boasts a main floor restaurant catering to many social and community functions, a fully stocked pro shop, and men's and ladies' locker rooms, washrooms, accounting office and meeting room downstairs.

THE FORMATIVE YEARS

The Messrs. Brown

"Bobby" and Arthur

A study of Qualicum Beach prior to 1980 finds Mr. R.A. Brown and Mr. Arthur Brown almost inextricably mixed together and sometimes even confused. In fact, they were quite different individuals and lived quite different lives.

R.A. Brown Jr., known as "Bobby" was born in Calgary, Alberta, in 1914, just a few weeks before the discovery of the Turner Valley Oilfield. Shortly after his father's company made its initial discovery, "Bobby" quit his studies at the University of Alberta and joined his father in a company called Brown, Moyer and Brown. Bob spent two years in the Canadian Navy beginning in 1943 and at the end of the war worked briefly in the Oil Controller's Department in Ottawa.

His chief impact on the Western Canadian business world occurred when he purchased Home Oil Company, which made major discoveries in the Western Canadian Sedimentary Basin. These important discoveries included Swan Hills, Virginia Hills, Carstairs, Harmatton-Elkton and Westward Ho.

Brown bought the original 'General Money House' on Crescent Road East in 1954 and, in that same year, hired Alex Smith and his wife to be the groundskeeper and housekeeper for the Brown property. Smith would later do double duty as the golf course superintendent. The house is easily recognizable since it is painted white, resembles a southern mansion and sits almost on Crescent Road East directly across from the sixth and seventh fairways. In 1955, Brown negotiated the purchase of the golf course for $25,000 with the Qualicum Beach Hotel Company having the right to lease it for four years. The golf club was leased to the hotel owners for an annual rent of $2,700 with an option to purchase for $45,000. The option was never exercised.

Alex Smith remained in the employ of R.A. Brown's family for close on thirty years until the Village of Qualicum Beach bought the Golf Course in 1981. Smith oversaw major improvements to the course in 1967-68, when a sprinkler system was installed for the fairways. Many trees were planted and general upgrading, including roto-tilling took place.

Today (2011) the house that R.A. Brown bought but was never a permanent family residence still stands proudly overlooking the golf course and beyond to the Strait of Georgia, a view that Mrs. Brown dearly loved, especially in her later years. It is now named Crown Mansion Boutique Hotel & Villas. Part of the original building has been remodelled and extended to include a number of villas and a restaurant.

Bob & Genevieve Brown

While this is essentially a history of the golf course in which R.A. Brown played a major role, Arthur Brown, his namesake, was also an integral part of the young community. Arthur was born in Ontario in 1910, and spent some time in Calgary working for the CPR, then moved to Vancouver where he managed the Vancouver Club until 1954. His wife Iris ran the Georgian Club for ladies, also in Vancouver, at the same time.

While he held that post in the city, Arthur was approached by Fred Sweet of Boultbee, Sweet, Walker and F.O. White to purchase the Qualicum Beach Hotel which had run into financial difficulties. He and his wife formed a company, the Qualicum Beach Inn Ltd., which bought the hotel for $105,000.

The hotel was considered luxurious when it was first constructed in 1913 by two contractors named Tinney and Humphrey; their foreman was Alec Fraser who built and lived in the white house across the street – 210 Crescent Road West. The house, once lived in by Mr. and Mrs. Dill, was donated to the town on her death and now houses the Qualicum Beach Hospice Society.

Over the years, guest needs and demands at the hotel changed. Larger rooms and private bathrooms became necessities. The hotel had not been constructed for winter use. To modernize and winterize would have been extremely expensive without any reasonable hope of repaying the cost.

Arthur Brown operated the hotel until his retirement in 1969 when the hotel was closed. It was taken down in 1972 and the property sold to a developer. The property was subdivided into 30 lots. The swimming pool became the foundation of one of the new houses.

Iris Brown died in 1985. In 1990, Arthur married Viola Burchitt from Biggar, Saskatchewan, who had served in a dual role at the hotel. She had been the receptionist and also worked in the office. Arthur died in 1997. In 2011, Viola now 97 years old, lives by herself, does her own cooking and housework and goes uptown on her electric scooter to do her own shopping, occasionally assisted by Barbara Penner, a good neighbour.

Arthur & Viola Brown

Robert A. Brown Jr.

My father, Robert A. (Bob) Brown, was born in Calgary, Alberta on 20 March, 1914, to Christina and Robert A. Brown Sr. I am quite sure he had no particular interest in the game of golf prior to coming out to Qualicum Beach in 1954 to negotiate the purchase of the Home Oil Company from James Lowery. He saw the Lowery home on Crescent Road East, and decided to make a bid for the whole works, company and house with surrounding 50-acre forest. When he told my mother, Genevieve (Genny) about his success, she was horrified at the thought of having to travel by plane, ferry and then gravel road to reach the new "summer house."

The lifestyle of an oilman in the 60s and 70s didn't leave much time for leisure, but his Qualicum Beach home was the one place where my dad relaxed. We were always told that the reason he decided in 1955 to purchase the golf course was to ensure that the magnificent view from the house would never be obscured by other homes. Over the years, of course, the view has been dramatically altered by the growth of trees planted when the course was re-styled in the 1960s. We three girls grew up thinking of the golf course as a sort of extension of the family acreage, available for evening walks, golf ball scavenging and other assorted mischief.

Both my parents golfed but my mother was the "natural" with a beautiful long-armed swing and a perfect follow through. My father, on the other hand, was a dreadful golfer as the game seemed to bring out in him all the qualities that made him such a good businessman – impatience, frustration with poor results, an inability to resist pulling his head up to keep his eye on the ball. This, in combination with a powerful barrel-chested physique, produced a golfer with a consistent (and vicious) hook on his drives and an uneven short game. When we were deemed old enough to steer a golf bag on a trolley, one of we three daughters was allowed to caddy occasionally. In the early days, this involved pulling the golf bag along (usually with clubs being spilled out as we went downhill), watching where the ball went and then clambering around in the rough or the gully trying to locate it before Dad got impatient and "took a drop." He had his own method of scorekeeping, which didn't seem to include penalty strokes at all! In all things, my father hated to concede defeat.

Each summer, our time as a family in Qualicum was precious – summers meant swimming, waterskiing, barbeques, tennis, golfing, fishing and building secret forts in the woods surrounding the house. Those same woods were the final resting place for many hundreds of golf balls that were misdirected the summer we got an auto-return golfing practice net. The idea of the copiously draped net was that you could hit a golf ball at it as hard as you liked and the net would absorb the energy of the ball, allowing it to fall harmlessly on the ground. Unfortunately, many of the balls never managed to hit the net, instead flying off at extreme angles into the woods. I am sure there are still hundreds of them littering the forest floor.

My father was given a replica 1903 Oldsmobile, fire engine-red with wooden-spoked narrow rubber wheels and an "aaooogah" horn mounted on the steering shaft. He named it "Genevieve" after our mother. It was a special summer treat for we three girls to be loaded onto the engine compartment on the back as Dad took us for an exhilarating ride across the active seventh fairway, smoke belching from the roaring two-stroke engine. Invariably, he would then try to get up to the top of Crescent Road – this required us to dismount from the now blistering hot engine cover and push on the rear end to get it over the crest. Going back down the long hill on the way home, "Genevieve" could get up to 28 mph (with a stiff tail wind)!

As we got older, we were desperate to be allowed to drive the golf cart, a brand new beige Toro with a gas engine. At a relatively tender age, while caddying for Dad, I inadvertently sent the new Toro golf cart hurtling over the edge of the cliff on the number 2 hole after a thrilling ride down the steep hill to the green. We had to get Alex Smith to bring the tractor mower to tow the cart back up the hill, which interrupted the game for some time. I do remember that my father expressed a good deal more concern for the welfare of the cart than for that of his daughter! Strangely, my sisters were asked to do most of the caddying for the remainder of that summer. We were paid the generous sum of twenty-five cents to caddy nine holes and fifty cents for eighteen. I am sure I made up for the deficit in my piggy bank with greater efforts in the gully, hunting stray balls and unbroken tees and selling them back to Alex Smith!

When my parents' friends joined them for a round of golf, we were told to look out for their approach along the seventh fairway so a member of the house staff could provide a thermos of liquid refreshments to the thirsty players. For years, I believed it was iced tea. The golfers always returned to the house in very good spirits. Alex Smith had a battered VW van he regularly drove on the golf course. Quite often, it was stocked with refreshing beverages and sandwiches, which he delivered to house guests as they made their way around the course. It was quite a surprise for regular members to see "bar and snack" service being offered and, on occasion, they availed themselves of the hospitality! It always delighted my dad to invite his guests to play golf during their stay at the house as he was very proud of the golf course.

Each September for a number of years, my father hosted an event known as the "Home Oil Freeloaders Weekend." This was a major undertaking with a guest list of up to 200 business leaders from all over North America attending a series of seminars, meetings and relaxing activities with our property being the central venue. There were no women allowed (that would certainly have changed in time!) and serious games of golf, tennis and a hard-fought fishing tournament provided the attendees with some healthy fresh air and physical exercise. In today's world, it would be called a "think tank." Needless to say, the outrageous accounts of intemperance and extreme conviviality were, if anything, understated in order to protect the good names of the participants! A commissioned bronze trophy was awarded to the competitor with the lowest golf score and the largest salmon – this trophy has recently been repatriated to the former Brown home and sits proudly displayed in the lobby of the now Crown Mansion.

There is a wonderful Home Oil Freeloaders weekend story about a local young lady who, while driving down Crescent Road East next to the fairway, had her windshield shattered by a golf ball. The startled young lady pulled over immediately and got out of her car to survey the damage. Two very solemn men approached her from mid-fairway. They asked her if her car had hit a golf ball to which she replied in the affirmative. One man said, "So, you admit it, then?" to which she repeated, "Yes." To her dismay, she was then "arrested" and conveyed with great ceremony to the poolside cabana behind the house. A "Kangaroo Court" was hastily convened, consisting of Freeloader guests who just happened to include a Chief Justice of the Supreme

THE FORMATIVE YEARS | 31

Court, two federal judges and several lawyers. To her horror, the hapless victim was charged with the offence of "Spherical obstruction and impeding the progress of a judicial ball" as it seemed that the golf ball in question had been driven off the sixth tee by the Chief Justice himself! It finally began to dawn on the frightened girl that she was the victim of a practical joke and although her guilt was never proved, she did stick around long enough to enjoy a couple of drinks in some very lofty company. Needless to say, the car windshield was repaired without charge to her!

My father used to enjoy his Qualicum breakfasts while seated at the bay window of the dining room, which overlooks the seventh fairway. He would watch as the golfers passed the house, usually making their approach shot to the green from right in front of him. Dad would be heard commenting, "Good shot" or "He isn't going to like that one" or even "I think that one landed in our hedge!" Our mother insisted that she would hear him saying under his breath, "Five bucks, five bucks, and another five bucks," as that was the green fee back in the day!

In the late sixties, Dad bought Mom a brand new electric golf cart – it even had a sunshade and she was delighted with it. We kids were, too, as we used it for great races through the woods, carrying up to ten passengers (if we and our friends all piled in on top of each other)! In later years, that same golf cart now old, battered and weary was further abused by all the grandchildren. They, too, drove it through the woods and trails before any of them had earned a proper driver's licence. Two of the grandchildren, Giles and Gareth, continue to enjoy playing golf on the Qualicum course when they are visiting family on the Island.

For many years after his death in 1972, my father's old Spalding golf clubs in their distinctive red and black leather golf bag sat in one of the garages next to the old electric cart. As I am only a little shorter than my dad was, his clubs were a good fit for me and I always felt a sort of connection with him when I used them on the course. They were hopelessly out of date with wooden club heads and heavy metal shafts. But, having played with those clubs for so many years, when I first played with a modern set with a "Big Bertha" driver, it almost felt like cheating. Although I haven't played much golf lately, I will always remember my one and only "Hole in one" on the second hole of the Qualicum Beach course.

Our Mother died in 2007, having spent the last 30 years of her life in Qualicum Beach. She continued to enjoy playing golf until the end of the seventies when her health prevented her from participating in the game she played so well. In 1993, my mother commemorated a stone cairn with a bronze plaque honoring my father, which had been commissioned by the Town of Qualicum Beach and the Golf Club. It sits close to where the first tee was then and to this day, whenever I drive up Memorial Avenue and pass by that spot, I think of Dad and smile. My sisters and I laid a memorial granite stone honouring our mother on the golf course in 2008. It is guarded by three Eastern maple trees, in memory of Genny Brown's birthplace in the Ottawa Valley and representative of her three daughters, Pamela, Lois and Carolyn. In these and so many other ways, I hope the Brown family will long remain a part of the Qualicum Beach Memorial Golf Course.

Author: Lois Brown (daughter)
July 2011

R.A. Brown Jr.'s House on Crescent Road East
This aerial photo of the Browns' house shows clearly the kind of forest growth that confronted those who carved the golf course out of the hinterland in the early 1900s. No modern day equipment was available. Today's sixth and seventh fairways are seen in the foreground.

Alexander Pirie Smith

Alexander Pirie Smith was born on December 31, 1915, in Vancouver, B.C. He was the second eldest of 5 brothers and one sister. Alexander joined the Navy in 1944 and served aboard the HMCS Merimishee, a minesweeper that patrolled our coastal waters from Tofino to Alaska. Alexander became a talented floral designer after the war and in 1954 while managing Brown's Florist (no relation to R.A. Brown) in Nanaimo he answered an ad in the newspaper for a caretaker at the Browns' estate in Qualicum Beach. He thought the long hours of being a florist was taxing on his young family. Little did he know what lay ahead!

Alex and Barb and their two children moved to Qualicum Beach in 1954 and eventually into the Browns' house in 1958. When Mr. Brown was in residence we all slept in a large room on the third floor of the Browns' house, now known as the Crown Mansion. We lived there until around 1969 then moved into our own home on the Island Highway overlooking Judges Row. My parents worked eighteen-hour days, seven days a week when the Browns were in residence and often would just get to sleep when something would transpire requiring one or both of them to attend to. It was not uncommon for the phone to ring at 1 am and Mr. Brown's pilot would tell us their ETA for Comox airport was 3 hours from then. The lights would go on, phone calls were made waking others up to come to help; and our entire family would race through the house making everything "just right."

In addition to caretaking the Brown property, Alex became the estate manager, provisioning for the family when they were in residence or acting as chauffeur; and for many years he also did all the cooking. While he was joined by my mom, who tirelessly took care of all the inside work, cooking was not my mom's talent. When I was eleven years old, I recall my father calling me into the kitchen and teaching me how to cook; "in self defense" he said. Dad and I spent many hours in the kitchen together, both at home and eventually at the golf course in the kitchen, cooking for the various golf tournaments. We all worked during the day and sometimes into the night prepping food for the weekend golf tournaments. Often it was just a quick shower and off we'd go again, keeping the routine of Dad's work duties. Many people reading this writing will recall the tournaments, the New Year's Eve parties, celebrating Alex's birthday, and feasting on one of his latest recipes. It is those times of the year that I miss my father the most.

It all started when Dad came into the room one day and announced, "Mr. Brown just made me the manager of the golf course." Dad knew nothing about golf … but he did know how to grow grass. Being the self-made man that he was, he set about learning the game and all that he could about the golf course business. Luckily, he had a natural talent for the sport, as he did for most things in his life; and he tirelessly threw himself into the routine of juggling all the work duties. The Browns had a boxer named Frisby; he was a bit of a character. Frisby would carouse around town all day then sit outside the post office waiting for a ride home. Part of Dad's regular routine was to pick Frisby up from the post office at 4 o'clock daily.

In the early 70s when Bob Brown passed away and the estate was taken over by a board of directors, lots of changes were made; decisions were made that sometimes didn't sit well with a lot of people including my father, but he was dedicated to the Brown family and to Mr. Brown's memory.

During the changes and improvements to the golf course, the whole community joined in, and we all picked a lot of rocks! As a kid growing up, my picking rocks on the fairway outside our home was a good way for my parents to keep track of me. Bless Dale Fabrick when he came along with his rock-picking machine!

The improvements and installation of the sprinkler system evolved into changing sprinklers all night long or checking on the pump in the gully, it was forever losing its prime. Many nights I recall my father coming home with his suit and tie covered in mud. If he didn't hear the pump come on he'd go down into the gully, in the dark, to investigate. My father often took on this task of changing sprinklers during the night himself so someone else could have a night off. It was many years later before the automated sprinkler system was installed.

As I recall, the only day my father did not go to the clubhouse was Christmas Day, or at least that was his plan so that day one could play golf for free. Of course, if a golfer didn't have clubs either our home phone would ring or someone would show up at our door and off he'd go to the clubhouse.

When the golf course was sold to the town of Qualicum Beach, he continued to work for the Brown family with only two changes to his job description. The colour of the truck changed from blue to brown, and the daily 4 o'clock passenger changed from Frisby to being my son, Iain, who always knew where to find Grandpa for a ride home.

I feel privileged to have been associated with all the people who worked at the golf course over the years, and those who played golf there with many returning year after year. The list is long, but you all know who you are, many of you became our extended family. We had so much fun. I am most privileged and proud that Alexander Pirie Smith was my Dad.

Author: Leslie Williams (daughter)
April 7, 2011

Dale Fabrick

Dale was born in Nanaimo and raised in Coombs, right next door to the "Goats on the Roof Market." He attended school in Coombs with the Gratton kids until grade six where his teacher was Mrs. Reddyhoff, "awesome teacher – best in the world!"

When he reached High School, life changed for Dale. He had the urge to get into the practical side of life. He loved Industrial Arts – never missed a class – but had little interest in French, compulsory by that time, and felt that his time could be better spent.

Dale said, "I missed eighty days of school in grade seven and passed." During his 'absences' he was employed running equipment for a logger. Along came grade nine. Dale showed up on opening day and registered. He sat down in class and asked himself the question, "What in heck am I doing here?" "I don't belong in this place." He gave all his stuff away to the other students – books, loose-leafs, pencils, and pens. Then he walked out. That was when he bought a tractor at age fourteen. "I also bought a Rotovator and did custom rotovating all around the district: Coombs, Parksville, Nanoose Bay and a few times in Nanaimo. Then to Port Alberni and rotovated some large market gardens."

He worked on the Qualicum Beach Golf Course, he stayed on with Alex Smith for three or four years looking after the lawns at the big house and helping on the golf course. He also worked at the stables. His Uncle Joe did market gardening and lived out past the Qualicum Beach Airport. He owned property from near the airport down almost to French Creek. That was his farm and it was a gorgeous piece of property.

Dale worked four years at the golf course in the early 1960s. He describes the fairways as burnt grass since this was before irrigation was installed.

The entire course was rotovated in 1964 and that was also when rock picking took place. There was a man named Karly Grasser who lived in Coombs and he came with his back-hoe and dug holes beside monster boulders – six to eight footers, which they could not move – and pushed them down in the holes and then they buried them. The three footers they buried themselves. Boulders like these were all over the golf course.

When they were done it was like a brand new golf course. The work took two years to complete. The rock picking was the biggest headache. They closed the course right after the long weekend in September of 1963. They were still picking rocks in 1964 and possibly into '65.

Dale Fabrick and his wife Tammy-Ann live at Agate Bay near Louis Creek, roughly fifty miles north of Kamloops, BC in the beautiful valley of the Adams River.

Qualicum Golf Course Gets a Face-Lifting

From: **The Islander Magazine**, May 1, 1966

(An edited version of an article written by Jeanette Forrester 10 times Ladies' Champion of Qualicum Beach Golf Club)

When manager Alex Smith announced the closing of the Qualicum Beach Golf Course late last summer, due to a full-scale renovation program, the lamenting had begun. For those who were on the staff of this popular layout, it became apparent, by the daily expressions from all and sundry of the deep interest displayed due to the foreseen preparations which ensued on this nine-hole paradise.

Survey work, rototilling and laying of the water pipes and sprinklers made great strides shortly after the course closed on September 20th.

Although the golf course was in dire need of fairway sprinklers and reseeding, much planning went into effect before the final word. This feat was far from easy to recarve a course, bring variety to some of the greens, diversity to the holes and strategy to the fairways. Although being blessed by having a creek, it took skilled engineers to make this project successful and meant a saving in water supply. Actually this was the main event.

Everything else fell into place as time went on. For a golf course so well situated and tremendously popular with tourists, its closure was heartbreaking as it meant taking a season's loss of green fees, cancellations and much correspondence. According to records, this little bonanza ranked tops on the island. The parking area lined up continually, beginning with Easter and right through the Labour Day weekend. But since the overall picture was to be considered, many a sacrifice had to be made.

Now, seven months later, the undertaking is beginning to fulfill a dream. The deep fairway undulations now evened off give the fairways a park like appearance, and even more so as tree planting progresses. Fairways have taken on a new sculptured look, which will go well with the plush greens. Keen interest sprang up with the pleasant weather as the local Men's Group came out in full force replete with rakes and rock pickers. Soon the fairways showed a great improvement.

Noticeable, too, was a Ladies' Group who volunteered to help with the rock picking of the small rocks that the machine was unable to collect. As soon as the rocks were eliminated from the fairways, seeding commenced.

These past few months have proved to the community that the golf course is the lifeblood of this tourist mecca, and unfavourable remarks have been met with scorn regarding its importance in business existence. If a Founder's Day is ever to be celebrated, then General Noel Money is entitled to head the list. For it was way back in 1912 under the impetus of that intrepid hotel operator that a full-scale 18-hole golf course was laid out. Some years later, it was reduced to nine holes, as demand for the valuable surrounding real estate was overwhelming.

The operation of these scenic links was then more difficult and horses were used for hauling freight and machinery from Nanaimo. East Indian and Chinese work crews numbering in the twenties were hired to clear the land and level the ground by hand. This was a painstaking ordeal, which was done with railroad irons with men at both ends, smoothing the soil and making other preparations before seeding. Present day techniques and modern machines were unheard of then. Walter Ford and Parker Belyea played a big role in land clearing

After the death of General Money, a large syndicate owned the course, with George

Walker as manager. In the mid 1940s J.A. Montgomery came to work as greenskeeper and D. MacLeod was golf professional who apparently did a lot of instructing in that capacity.

After MacLeod's death, the genial Montgomery became head of the Pro Shop. He served faithfully and well over a long period of time and became a legend with the golfing public. When 'Monty' retired, Jon Leyne became golf professional and assisted with the present day renovations. The other member of the pro shop staff was Jeanette Forrester who gained much of her experience from ' Monty' in dealing with the golfing public.

Due to the past connection between the Qualicum Beach Inn and the golf course many guests are still under the impression that the two are joined. Numerous golfers arrive from Victoria each season as well as other parts of the continent and the Qualicum Beach Inn has been accepted as their second home.

The golf course is still lacking in buildings as the presently used clubhouse and Pro Shop belong to the Inn. A modern clubhouse will be a future 'must' to go with the newly renovated course and it is then that the Qualicum Beach Golf Course will stand on its own feet and take on a new meaning.

If a golf course gained such popularity in the past with its adverse conditions, it will most certainly have a great future with its new lush turf, smooth fairways and some of the best greens on the Island. It is already pleasing to the eye and a year hence it will most definitely be a scene-stealer.

From: The Islander Magazine, May 1, 1966

The Inn, as magnificent on its hilltop as the view it has, closed its doors Monday.

From: **The Qualicum Beach Progress,**
Wednesday, October 1, 1969

The Day the Qualicum Beach Hotel Closed.

Classic charm of Qualicum Beach Inn will be long remembered by those who visited it throughout it's 57 year history.

Dining Room, Qualicum Beach Hotel.

THE FORMATIVE YEARS | 39

Qualicum Beach Memorial Golf Course

Purchased by Town of Qualicum Beach 1981

Arthur N. Skipsey
Mayor of Qualicum Beach 1978 – 1990

Council members serving with Arthur N. Skipsey were:
J.E. Collins, E.W. Baker, K.C. Keilty, J. Langton, and Leo Klees, Clerk/Administrator

Arthur Skipsey tells us part of what happened:

Arther N. Skipsey

"As the story goes, one day a surveyor's peg appeared in front of Bobby Brown's house – this immediately prompted Mr. Brown to purchase the golf course in 1955 for $25,000.00 and he immediately installed his personal estate manager, Alexander Smith, as manager of the golf course. Alex Smith remained in this position for nearly thirty years. By 1980, the great rumour of the time was that Block Bros Real Estate had purchased the golf course and they planned to subdivide it; an idea that haunted the townsfolk because to lose their golf course would be a major catastrophe. We had often talked about this prospect during council meetings – could we purchase the golf course, and if we did would we need to purchase the rest of the Brown property in anticipation of future expansion of the course? The conclusion we came to was, no we did not; to do so would destroy this natural forested area in order to have the full eighteen holes.

Council also made the decision that if they were to purchase the golf course they would not manage it; they would get the golfers themselves to do that. We had done the same sort of thing with the lawn bowlers. We assisted the lawn bowlers by giving them a portion of the Community Park and they ran their own show.

Mr. Evans Wasson, a lawyer who spent his summers at 225 Crescent Road West in Qualicum Beach, brokered the purchase deal for Council. Mr. Wasson had connections with the management group for Home Oil in Calgary, Alberta. Together they finalized the legal aspects. However, only part of the transaction had been completed.

Mr. Leo Klees, the Village Clerk, approached Mr. Wasson to see if the Brown estate would sell the golf course to the Village. Mr. Wasson was himself in favor of this purchase and he presented it to the Brown family. Mr. Klees acted as the chief negotiator for the Village and was able to bring the proposal to a successful conclusion. Eventually, a price of one million dollars was agreed upon. Mrs. Brown, the immediate beneficiary, could have received a lot more for the sale of this property through real estate developers, but she recognized that maintenance of this land, as a golf course was critical to preserving the ambience and character of the Village of Qualicum Beach.

Some years prior to the golf course purchase, the Village had purchased the Grandview Cottages and Camp on the Old Island Highway, just west of the Shady Rest. The purchase price involved a land swap plus cash to mortgage. The segment on the south side of the highway was sold for $525,000 to a developer. The developer planned a terraced building very similar to the current Crystal Terraces plan. They rushed out to put in the on grade foundation to take advantage of a government incentive called MURB (Multi Unit Residential Building).

The sale agreement was that, when the project was built, the Village would develop the beach property. Unfortunately, the developer went bankrupt. The interest rate was 21% so they could neither finance nor market the property.

Meanwhile, the north or waterside of the highway had been levelled and added to the Village's seawall property. Thus, the Village of Qualicum Beach was able to provide the one million dollars for the golf course purchase without raising taxes, by using the $525,000 together with reserve from the sale of lots in town and surpluses.

And so now the Village of Qualicum Beach owned the golf course land and collected yearly rent plus one half of the profit, i.e. the surplus of revenue over expenses. The arrangement at that time was that the golf club would pay the Village $25,000 annually for the lease of the property and any profits would be split 50/50. We would then meet with the club once a year to discuss any changes they may be considering regarding the management of the club.

Pat Gadd's local construction company built a log clubhouse in 1970 on the corner of Memorial Avenue and Crescent Road. The building served the club well until a new facility was opened overlooking the ocean in 2008."

TELEPHONE 752-6923

The Corporation of the Village of Qualicum Beach
INCORPORATED 1942

P.O. BOX 130
QUALICUM BEACH, B.C.
V0R 2T0

Resolution — Purchase of Qualicum Golf Course
1981.07.06

Moved and Seconded that:

"The Mayor and Clerk be authorised to excecute an offer to purchase the Qualicum Beach Golf Course from Rabsco Investments Limited for the purchase price of $1,000,000.00 with terms as set out in the agreement."

Resolution Carried

Certified a true copy of Resolution
passed by Council of the Corporation
of the Village of Qualicum Beach
July 6, 1981

L. Klees – Clerk

THE CORPORATION OF
THE VILLAGE OF QUALICUM BEACH
P.O. BOX 130 PHONE 752-6723
QUALICUM BEACH, B.C. V0R 2T0

No. 2186

June 11 1981

PAY TO THE ORDER OF   VILLAGE OF QUALICUM BEACH $5,000 and 00 cts   DOLLARS $ 5,000.00

Macleod, Dixon
Barristers & Solicitors
1500 Home Oil Tower
324 - 8th Avenue S.W.
Calgary, Alberta T2P 2Z2

THE CORPORATION OF
THE VILLAGE OF QUALICUM BEACH

CANADIAN IMPERIAL BANK OF COMMERCE
QUALICUM BEACH, B.C. V0R 2T0

MAYOR
TREASURER

THE CORPORATION OF
THE VILLAGE OF QUALICUM BEACH

DETACH AND RETAIN THIS STATEMENT
THE ATTACHED CHEQUE IS IN PAYMENT OF ITEMS DESCRIBED BELOW

Re: Golf Course Purchase

TOWN OF QUALICUM BEACH

The Covenant

The Qualicum Beach Memorial Golf Course, and our community, have been blessed by people with vision and community spirit!

First in 1913 when a visionary opened this golf course, and on August 31, 1981, when the Council and Administration of the day showed great insight and courage when they purchased the golf course from the Brown family for $1 million.

The Brown family showed vision too, by co-operating in fulfilling this unique arrangement, including registering a Restrictive Covenant on the land to ensure the land would never be used for any purpose other than a golf course or public park.

The Restrictive Covenant, registered in the Land Title Office on July 21, 1981 under No. K74555, just before the land was sold to the Town, is an agreement where the property owner, Rabsco Investments Limited (a company of the Brown family), was the Grantor and the Grantee. The six-page document is comprised primarily of preamble at the beginning, and three pages of legal descriptions of the property at the end, but the purpose is described in the profound and meaningful clauses in the centre:

> *NOW THEREFORE the Grantor hereby covenants with the Grantee to the intent that the burden of this Covenant may run with and bind the Golf Course Lands and every part thereof and to the intent that the benefit hereof may be annexed to and run with the Benefited Lands, not to use the Golf Course Lands for any purpose other than a golf course or public park;*
>
> *THE GRANTOR FURTHER COVENANTS with the Grantee to the intent that the burden of this Covenant may run with and bind the Burdened Lands and every part thereof, and to the intent that the benefit hereof may be annexed to and run with the Benefited Lands not to construct or place or allow to be constructed or placed upon the Burdened Lands any building, structure or improvement that would alter the Burdened Lands from their present natural state.*

Further clauses in the Restrictive Covenant confirm that nothing in the covenant shall prohibit the Golf Course Lands from being maintained as a golf course or public park. The Restrictive Covenant also goes on to confirm that future owners of the land shall not have any power to waive or vary or release the Restrictive Covenant, or any parts of it. We congratulate the visionaries of yesterday, and the caretakers of that vision, the Golf Club, who are today and will be for many years to come, partners with the Town of Qualicum Beach as we maintain not only a living piece of history but a vibrant asset in our community - the Qualicum Beach Memorial Golf Course!

Teunis Westbroek, Mayor
Town of Qualicum Beach

On behalf of Councillors Barry Avis, Kent Becker, Mary Brouilette & Jack Wilson

National 'Communities in Bloom' & 'Floral' Award Winner

THE CORPORATION OF THE VILLAGE OF QUALICUM BEACH
P.O. Box 130 Phone 752-6723
Qualicum Beach, B.C. V0R 2T0

No. 2357
August 31 19 81

Pay Nine Hundred & Ninety-five Thousand ---------- 00 Dollars $ 995,000.00
To the Order of: Rabsco Investments Ltd.,
Suite 530-880 Douglas Street,
Victoria, B.C.

CANADIAN IMPERIAL BANK OF COMMERCE
QUALICUM BEACH, B.C. V0R 2T0

THE CORPORATION OF THE VILLAGE OF QUALICUM BEACH

MAYOR
TREASURER

DETACH AND RETAIN THIS STATEMENT
THE ATTACHED CHEQUE IS IN PAYMENT OF ITEMS DESCRIBED BELOW

Qualicum Beach Golfcourse Purchase

THE FORMATIVE YEARS

Personalities

Personalities

Qualicum Beach Caddy Master Fred Westnedge – on left.

Personalities, national and international, discovered the pleasures of Qualicum Beach's elegant hotel, golf course and salmon fishing from Bing Crosby to The King of Siam.

Almost all of the caddies who worked Qualicum Beach during the summers were from Victoria and other large centres. A 'Cheapskate List' posted in the Qualicum caddy shack identified players who didn't pay the going rates – fifty cents for nine holes, one dollar for eighteen. The caddies refused to take their bags. English born Fred Westnedge, while in his early teens, was Qualicum Beach's caddy master and he dealt directly with celebrities and aristocrats who visited the posh Vancouver Island haven during the late 1920s and early 1930s. Westnedge earned sixty dollars per month, plus room and board, and free golf and tennis.

"My accent helped me get the job," said Westnedge. "The entire staff in the hotel was very, very English." He remembers serving Zane Grey, Edgar Rice Burroughs, Dr. Davidson and Major-General Francis Arthur Sutton.

Dr. Davidson, a Titanic survivor who wore a neck brace, was the only medical man in town. One day a hotel bellhop rushed out on the course to find the good doctor whose services were urgently required at the scene of a nearby automobile accident. Dr. Davidson anxiously asked the foursome at the ninth tee if his group could play through!

Major-General Sutton, a flamboyant soldier of fortune, found his way to Qualicum Beach from Vancouver, where he arrived in 1927 and purchased the Rogers Building and Portland Island in the Gulf of Georgia. The English adventurer had lost his right arm at Gallipoli during the First World War and became known as "One-Arm" Sutton. He had an artificial limb but the handicap didn't prevent him from playing golf. Do you look after things around here? Sutton enquired of the young caddy master while preparing to debut at Qualicum. "Yes sir," replied Westnedge. "Well hold on to this for safekeeping, laddie," said Sutton, removing the limb and handing it to the startled youngster.

Arv Olson, BACKSPIN

The Prince of Wales visited the village in 1919, but it is not recorded whether he had a game of golf. He did visit convalescing veterans at the Qualicum Beach Inn, however.

There followed a succession of Governors General of Canada.

Lord and Lady Byng came first, followed by Lord and Lady Bessborough, then the Willingdons who actually visited twice. Also included in this Vice-Regal chain of visits were: Lord Tweedsmuir, The Earl of Athlone, Viscount Alexander of Tunis and Vincent Massey.

Not many island golf courses have been graced by royalty but, in the 1920s the King and Queen of Siam appeared here while the course layout still required golfers to hit across Memorial Avenue. One day a local lad in his new Chevrolet was driving his prized automobile back from the beach over the road, which crossed one of the fairways. The latch on the hood of his new car came undone so he got out to fix it, not realizing he was still on the golf course.

Suddenly a voice yelled at him, "Make way for the King of Siam!" Imagine his chagrin, the redness of his face, when, barely bothering to look up, he shouted back, "Oh sure, I'm the Duke of Buccleugh, myself!" only to discover that it really was the King of Siam and his retinue waiting impatiently to pass through. The Queen was not with him. She was in her room at the hotel, knitting and playing with her pet kitten, which travelled with her in a basket. Those who remember, say that the cat was not a Siamese!

Parksville/Qualicum Beach PROGRESS

Qualicum Beach Inn, built in 1913, operated as a hotel until 1915 when the government took it over as a convalesence base for soldiers until 1919 when it reverted. Photo taken in 1916.

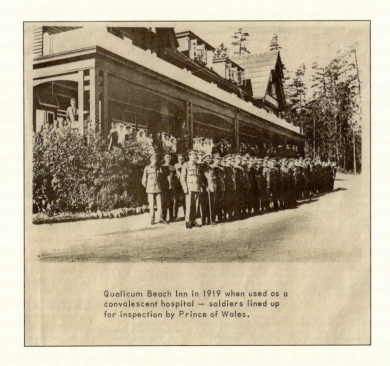

Qualicum Beach Inn in 1919 when used as a convalescent hospital — soldiers lined up for inspection by Prince of Wales.

PERSONALITIES

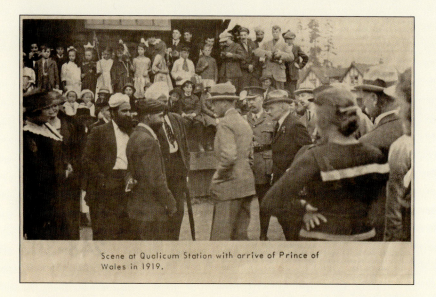
Scene at Qualicum Station with arrive of Prince of Wales in 1919.

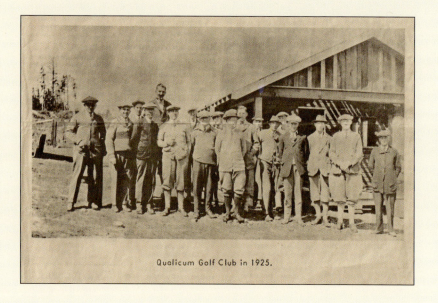
Qualicum Golf Club in 1925.

Bob Hope and Charlie McAllister
The McAllister family owned and operated the Sunset Inn from 1941 – 1953. The Inn stood on the corner of Memorial and Crescent Road E directly across from the present 3rd green and was a favourite lodging spot for the many visiting golfers.

48 | PERSONALITIES

A Legend

Ernie Bentley, besides being an extremely fine golfer, was also a humble man who rubbed shoulders with all of the greats in North American golf between the years 1945 to 1985. He was an amateur, a contemporary of Moe Norman, Nick Weslock, Gerry Kesselring and Gary Cowan.

Emily and Ernie Bentley

Ernie played in six Canadian Opens and made the cut three times. His typical summer schedule consisted of playing in tournaments (10 or 12 per year) in Ontario, Quebec and New York State. He has said that the prizes he won helped furnish the Bentley home. His favorite course was the Weston Golf Club in Toronto.

Ernie's caddies were his children as they grew up and latterly his wife Emily was almost always 'on the bag.' She carried the clubs, and was in that role when he won his last club championship at Qualicum Beach in the year 2000 at age seventy-seven. It is fair to say that the Bentleys caddied for each other whenever the occasion arose. The great 'secret' of Ernie's swing was the momentary pause at the top – it is something that the really outstanding golfers of any age have either come by naturally or perfected through practice.

Consider Ernie's overall record;

22 Club Championships –
- 13 at Weston Golf Club
- 7 at Cherry Downs
- 1 at Ottawa Hunt Club
- 1 at Qualicum Beach Memorial Golf Club

2 Ontario Champion of Champions and represented that province on the Willingdon Cup Team. 8 Holes in one; 7 in Toronto, 1 in Hawaii.

During his peak playing years, Ernie weighed 150 pounds and stood five feet seven inches tall.

The above caption reads – shown in puckish mood as they played the final tournament of golf for the year at Qualicum Golf Club are top row, left to right – Mrs. Corfield, Dr. Livesay, Peter Barr, Mrs. Montgomery, Mrs. Fred Parker, Charlie McAllister, Mrs. Brion, Mrs. Mary Goard, Mrs. Campbell, Mrs. Patterson, Mrs. Gibson and Hugh Reid, Center row, left to right – Mrs. Peter Barr, Roy Crawley, D'Arcy Bacon, Jack Anderson, Mrs. George Irvine, Bottom row, left to right – Jimmy Muir, Mrs. Crawley, Bill Reid, Dr. Montgomery, Mr. Gibson, Mrs. Edna Dugan, D. Fraser.

Jim Stephen, teeing up, emerged as junior golf champion at Qualicum Beach Saturday, beating out defending champ Neil Higgs in a "sudden death" play-off. Taking part in the tournament were (left to right) Craig Jenkins, Ross Logan, Bruce McKay (low net winner), Rick Walz, Rory Johnston, Jim Stephen, Neil Higgs, Leslie Leyne, Ted Laver and Steve Knight. Neil Higgs won the Harvey Dash Memorial Shield for match play. (Progress Photo, September 10, 1969)

Steve Watson and his parents Dorothy and John Watson – May 1983 – Steve held the course record at "62" as recorded July 19, 1983. In more recent years, Steve has won the Qualicum Beach Men's Amateur Tournament both in 1996 and 2010.

At 98, BUS Broatch still prefers to walk the golf course.

CONTINUED FROM PAGE A32

July 2008

Three amigos sharing laughs on the links

"Morning Bus," one golfer smiled on the way past, adding "he's our poster boy."

Bus, it should be noted, was also a good curler back in the day — he represented B.C. as lead at the brier in Toronto in 1936.

Asked if he plans on hanging up his clubs anytime soon, the senior shook his head and said, "No. Not as long as I can go out there and Jim will let me play with them. As long as I'm able."

Bus, it turns out, is one part of what some have dubbed the three amigos — including Ray Zoost, and Jim Weeks — who have been playing together for years. Bus and his good pal Ray, a retired mill worker, have been golfing together in QB every week since the 1970s. Zoost, who turns 95 in September and is still sharp as a tack, has had hip replacement surgery and uses a cart.

Weeks, 70, came on board and rounded out the threesome 10 years ago.

These days Ray and Jim go out at 7 a.m. for the first nine holes. Ray leaves, and Bus and Jim carry on for the back nine.

"Jim's a real good golfer — he puts up with both of us," Bus chuckled of Weeks.

"He's a prince," Ray added.

"Absolutely," Jim said when asked if he enjoys his time with Bus and Ray. "Two best guys on the course I tell 'ya."

Qualicum Beach Memorial Golf Club head pro Ross Mantell is very familiar with the three amigos.

"Great guys ... people know who they are around here that's for sure."

AT 98, BUS Broatch still prefers to walk the golf course.

PERSONALITIES | 51

Peter Barr re-captures Golf Championship title

PETER BARR
... regains title

Qualicum Beach – Smooth-stroking Peter Barr of Qualicum Beach topped an entry field of 59 golfers in the men's division of the three-day annual Qualicum Beach Inn Golf Tournament here on the holiday weekend.

Runner-up in the championship flight was G. Burgess of Courtenay.

Burgess was winner of the event last year while Pete Barr captured the 1960 tournament laurels.

Low gross winner was A. Omelus of Vancouver while winner of the low net was former local resident, Hughie Reid, now a resident of Victoria.

Miss D. Andrew, of Vancouver, topped a field of 37 in the ladies' segment of the tournament. Runner-up was Miss M. Russell, also of Vancouver, Mrs. J. Munro of Victoria captured the low gross score while Mrs. R. A. Brown, Calgary, won the low net silverware.

Wednesday, May 23, 1962

MEN'S CHAMPIONSHIP TROPHY was presented to Ralph Forrester, left, at recent banquet meeting of Qualicum Beach Golf Club. Peter Barr, at the right, and President R. H. Hodgson made the awards to all winners during the ceremonies.

From: **The Parksville - Qualicum Beach Newspaper,**
Wednesday, March 7, 1956

FOUNDED 1916

PHONE 752-6312

Qualicum Beach Memorial Golf Course
Box 1633, QUALICUM BEACH, B.C. V0R 2T0

THE MOST SCENIC GOLF COURSE ON VANCOUVER ISLAND

LOCAL RULES
ALL PLAY GOVERNED BY R.C.G.A. RULES EXCEPT AS MODIFIED BELOW

- **WHITE STAKES:** Out of Bounds — No. 2-3-5-6-7-8-9
- **RED STAKES:** Lateral Water Hazard - NO. 6
- **STAKED TREES:** Or protective netting interfering with stance or swing - FREE DROP two club lengths no nearer the hole.
- **POWER LINES:** No. 5. A ball striking the power line (in bounds) may be replayed without penalty. (The second ball must be played.)
- **DRESS CODE:** Must be observed at all times.
- **SMALL CHILDREN & PETS:** Are not allowed on the course.

PLAYERS USE GOLF COURSE AND CARTS AT THEIR OWN RISK

PLEASE } Keep up to the group golfing ahead of you. Keep all carts 20 feet from all greens and tees. Replace divots. Repair ball marks. Rake sand traps.

STEVE CIKALUK — PRO-MANAGER
RORY JOHNSTONE — COURSE SUPERINTENDENT

Qualicum Beach Memorial Golf Course
VANCOUVER ISLAND, B.C. CANADA

279

HOLE	1	2	3	4	5	6	7	8	9	OUT
YARDAGE	151	136	468	222	296	293	450	452	310	2778
MEN'S HDCP.	15	17	1	13	9	7	3	5	11	
MEN'S PAR	3	3	5	3	4	4	5	5	4	36
B	2.95	2.88	4.59	3.31	3.58	3.57	4.50	4.51	3.65	33.54
LADIES' PAR	3	3	5	4	4	4	4	5	4	36
LADIES' HDCP.	15	17	1	13	11	7	5	3	9	
YARDAGE	151	136	468	222	296	293	350	452	227	2595

NATIONAL COURSE RATING
MEN'S REGULAR - White-Red 66 / SHORT - White-Red 64
CLGA REGULAR (White - Red)... 67 / LONG (Yellow Tees 7-18)... 68 / LONG (Yel. Tees 7-9-16-18)... 69

INITIALS	10	11	12	13	14	15	16	17	18	IN	TOTAL	HDCP	NET
	139	136	468	222	296	293	468	452	280	2754	5532		
	16	18	2	14	10	8	4	6	12				
	3	3	5	3	4	4	5	5	4	36	72		
	2.96	2.88	4.59	3.31	3.58	3.57	4.59	4.51	3.50	33.43	66.87		
PLAYERS	3	3	5	4	4	4	4	5	4	36	72		
	16	18	2	14	12	8	6	4	10				
	139	136	468	222	296	293	350	452	227	2583	5178		

Date _____ Attested by _____ Scored by _____

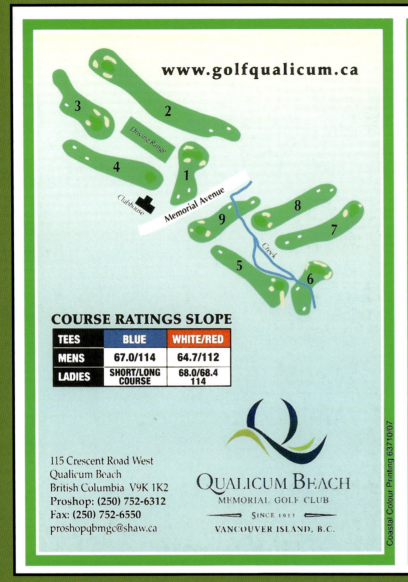
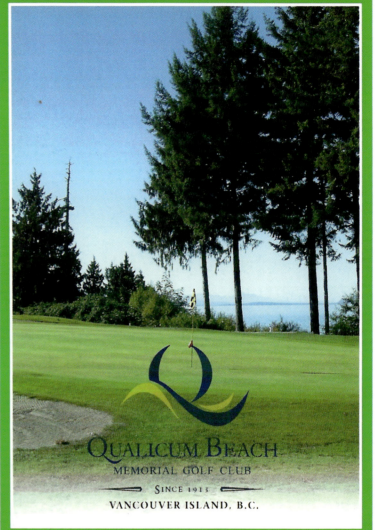

HOLE	1	2	3	4	5	6	7	8	9	OUT	INITIALS	10	11	12	13	14	15	16	17	18	IN	TOT		
Blue	144	507	222	323	295	140	397	457	340	2825		144	507	175	323	295	140	397	426	340	2747	5572		
Yardage (Mens)	135	502	192	295	285	118	345	447	315	2634		126	502	160	318	285	127	384	421	315	2638	5272		
Men's Handicap	15	1	5	13	11	17	3	9	7			18	6	14	12	10	16	4	2	8			HCP	NET
PAR M/L	3	5	3/4	4	4	3	4	5	4	35/36		3	5	3	4	4	3	4	4/5	4	34/35	69/71		
+/-																								
Yardage (Ladies)	135	502	222	295	285	95	345	447	226	2552		126	439	160	318	285	113	384	421	283	2529	5081		
Ladies' Handicap	17	1	15	9	7	13	5	3	11			18	2	16	8	10	14	4	6	12				

ORDER OF PLAY: FRONT 9 — White Markers BACK 9 — Red Markers

DATE _____

SCORER _____

ATTESTED BY _____

LOCAL RULES

- Please keep power and pull carts 30 feet from tees and greens.
- Maximum - 4 Players per group.
- Please Replace divots, Repair ball marks, and Rake sand traps.
- R.C.G.A. Rule of Golf govern play.
- Out of bounds - White Stakes: 2, 4, 5, 7, 8, 9.
- Lateral Water Hazard - Red Stakes: 5, 8.
- Water Hazard - Yellow Stakes: 9.

"Golfers are responsible for all balls hit off the property."

One of many renovations on the clubhouse at the corner of Memorial and Crescent in the '80s.

1981 – First Elected Board of Directors at Qualicum Beach Memorial Golf Course. Back row, left to right – Fred Boughen, Art Bridge (President) Drake McCrea. Front row, left to right – Maureen Bridge, Verna Bennett.

The Cost of Golf in Qualicum Beach in 1982

	Members	Annual Fee	Initiation Fee
Men	91	$275.00	$100.00
Ladies	24	$255.00	$100.00
Couples	97	$440.00	$150.00
Family	5	$495.00	$150.00
Juniors	35	$ 70.00	
Winter	14	$100.00	

Total playing membership: 376

The Cost of Golf in Qualicum Beach in 2012

	Members	Annual Fee	Initiation Fee
Men	237	$1,000.00	$1,500.00
Ladies	144	$1,000.00	$1,500.00
Juniors	10	$ 150.00	
Winter	22	$ 495.00	

Total playing membership: 413

Shirley Elliott accepted the Club Championship Trophy at the annual meeting of the Ladies Club of Qualicum Beach Memorial Golf Club. Runner-up was Margaret Thompson. Low net winner in the championship was Gerry Phillippe. Joyce Hope and Joan Jeffs tied for runners-up.

Other trophy winners: Rose Bowl, Lois Kaye; runner-up, Bev Reber; consolation, Joan Jeffs. Mary Goard trophy: Ev Scanlon, Sheilagh Larsen and June Aoki, tied for runners-up.

Maureen Bridge – six times Ladies' Champion 1972, 1974 thru 1977, 1982.

Margaret Thompson co-holds the record number of wins in the Qualicum Beach Ladies' Club Championship with a total of 10 wins.

Mikey Aylesworth – six times Ladies' Champion 2000-2006.

58 | PERSONALITIES

B30 - The Parksville-Qualicum Beach NEWS, Tuesday, November 5, 1991

Qualicum ladies wrap up golf season with awards ceremony

Two days after a record snowfall the Qualicum Beach Ladies 18-Hole Golf Club packed up their clubs with an awards day Nov. 2

Here are the 1991 season winners.

Rose Bowl (26-40 handicap): Winner Mary Varney, runner up Lois Hayward, consolation flight winner Kaye Kennedy.

Mary Goard Trophy (36 holes, low net): Winner Helen Williams (125), runner up Cathie Chambers (132).

Money Memorial Trophy (36 holes low net): Winner Helen Williams (130), runner up Joy Boyes.

Club Championship (54 holes-low gross-low net): Low gross winner Bev Lasure (259), runners up Daureen Evans (261) and Margaret Thompson (262). Low net winner Kaye Kennedy (212), runners up Joan Prendergast (213) and Sheilagh Larsen (215).

Bronze Trophy (19-39 handicap): Winner Shielagh Larsen, consolation flight winner Cathy Chambers and first flight winner Ronnie Wood.

Captain's Trophy (ecclectic): Low gross winner Daureen Evans (64), low net winner Doris Receiver (43).

Jowsey Trophy (putts-best to average): Trophy winner Joan Prendergast (13.7) runners up Miriam Fraser (14.9), Bev Lasure (14.9) Marg Thompson (14.9).

Muriel Reid Trophy (handicap reduction): Winner Daureen Evans (20 per cent, 20-14), runner up Nancy Hindmarch (13.64 per cent, 34-28).

Birdie Tree: Winner Doris Receveur (11 birdies).

Polly Putter: Winners Joan Prendergast, Lois Hayward, Tenna Johnston and Joy Sutherland. Each had 11 putts.

CLGA Pin Award: Winner Daureen Evans, runner up Joan Jeffs.

AUGUST 27, 1997

Lasure takes QBMGC ladies club championship for the third time

Bev Lasure, for the third time, is the Club Champion of the Ladies Club at Qualicum Beach Memorial Golf Club. Her first win was in 1985 and then 1991. Her score for 54 holes was 260.

First runner-up is nine-time winner Margaret Thompson with 272. Second place runner-up is Joan Bodie with 289. Low net winner for the 54 holes is Sheilagh Larsen with 207. Following her is Shirley Elliott with 214 and Blanche Barrett with 221. Low gross winner for regular play was Bev Lasure with 87, Larsen, 89, Joan Jeffs, 95, Thompson, 96 and Yvette Edgar, 102.

Low net winners were Ev Scanlan, 71, Joan Bodie, 72 and Ruth Brodie, 73. Birdies were scored by Dorothy Boyd and Sheilagh Larsen.

Double Champion – Ted Powell

At age 72, most golfers probably feel that their lowest scoring days are behind them – and this is realistic for many. Ted reached age 72 in 1994, soon after the brand new Glengary (currently named Pheasant Glen) Golf Course opened in Qualicum Beach. He became a member and also Men's Champion. This was before the course underwent a radical new layout design. Ted shot 66 to win the Championship, which at that time was played over 18 holes.

Meanwhile, he had been honoured and elected Captain at Qualicum Beach Memorial Golf Club, a position to which he gave distinguished service. The Men's Championship at the venerable club had always been over 36 holes and two days. The 72-year-old Powell shot 71 both days and so achieved the great double honour of being Champion at both clubs.

A feat that may not be equaled!

For the record:

Ted's lowest scores:
- 9 holes at Qualicum Beach – 31
- 18 holes at Qualicum Beach – 67
- 18 holes at Glengarry – 64

Holes in one: 4

Preparing for the Qualicum Beach Men's Amateur Tournament 1993 – this putting green still exists; the club house was demolished in 2005.

Ladies' Senior Button's wind-up party in Port Alberni 1998 Back row, left to right – Verna Bennet, Margaret Thomson, Ethel Simpson, Francis Wilson, Joan Pirie, Pat Crier; Front row, left to right – Marguerite Bowness, Elsie Webb, Joan Jeffs, Helen Williams, Lynn Gordon, Shirley McGill, Bev Lasure.

The Qualicum Beach Men's Amateur Tournament 1993 preparations – The car in the background was sitting just off the #1 tee box at that time and was the "Hole in One" prize.

Ross giving last minute instruction to the members and guests at the Adam & Eve Tournament 2011. There were 50 players, playing alternate shot. Lynn Bailey and Alex Briden won the tournament.

PERSONALITIES | 61

Peter Barr

My father, Peter Barr, was an excellent golfer. He learned to play at Gleneagles in West Vancouver when he was a young boy living in Horseshoe Bay. At the age of 18 in 1940, he scored his first, and only, hole in one for which he received a certificate from Canadian Golfer and a box of Canada Dry ginger ale.

Peter could have become a professional golfer, but World War II intervened. He lied about his age, joined the Lord Strathcona Horse, and was shipped overseas to fight in the Italian Campaign as a tank driver. He was one of the lucky ones that returned home.

He married my mother, Joyce, in 1947 and in 1949 they moved permanently to Qualicum Beach to help my grandmother, Flora La Marre, run the Van Isle Resort. He resumed golfing at the Qualicum Beach Golf Course where he played until 1967.

My father first earned his living as a logger working at "Camp" up the Horne Lake Road. In 1957 the Ministry of Education was recruiting journeymen from the forest industry to become Industrial Arts teachers, so my father applied. He attended summer school and got his first teaching position in September 1958, in Alert Bay, B.C. We moved there just for the school season and retuned home to Qualicum Beach on school holidays. He then moved to A.W. Neill School in Port Alberni, then to Parksville and eventually to Qualicum Beach High School in 1969 where he taught grades 11 and 12.

Annually, on the May 24th weekend from 1950 till the mid 60s, he played in the Qualicum Beach Inn Tournament, which he won more than once. Friends and relatives would come for the weekend to play including Evan Wolfe, who later was to become Social Credit Minister of Finance in Bill Vander Zalm's government.

Peter was also Club Champion 7 times, his name engraved on the trophy still on display in the clubhouse.

Around 1966, while still owned by Robert Brown, the golf course underwent a major renovation to install irrigation. We were all involved as a family and spent weekends raking stones off the fairways. We even contributed trees from our property that were planted for new landscaping. However, something happened between my father and others involved at the time. There was a "falling out" and my father quit the club. From that day on, he joined the Nanaimo Golf Club and never played again at Qualicum.

Peter's golf ended permanently by an unfortunate accident at school where he cut the tendons in the two middle fingers on his left hand. His fingers never healed properly so he could no longer hold a golf club.

He retired from teaching in 1976 at the age of 55, but his health was deteriorating from a series of minor strokes. He died of a massive stroke at the age of 57.

Author: Terry Murray (daughter)
March 17, 2011

Inter-club competition at Sunnydale Golf Course 1984

Front row, left to right – George Hollins, Dick Bailey, Bill Hilton, Hank Bennett, Ray Morris, Pat Collins, Steve Cikaluk, Pro. Back rows, left to right – Art Bridge, Al Craven, Bob Motherwell, Ted Powell, William Crowther, George Rhodes, Art Chapman, Scotty McVicar, Wilf Mitchell, Dick Brandback, Darryl Vossler, Jim Hunter, Bernie Ktekstab, Ray Zoost, Harold Engleson, Fred Hayward.

The Map Makers –

Left to right – Fred Parker, Bert Parker, Jack Parker.

There is a series of five different golf course layouts included in this book. Careful study will show the reader that the original layout designed by Vernon Macan in 1913 has changed over the years. The map makers pictured here spent many hours putting this series together and hopefully readers will find their efforts informative.

For example, the **1913-1949** version shows two of the nine holes played across Memorial Avenue, which at that time was little more than a cart track. This practice stopped in 1949 when too many car headlights were smashed by errant golf balls! At this stage there were no bunkers on the golf course.

1949-1970 The location of the clubhouse and Caddie Shack can be seen next to what is now the third tee box. A major improvement took place in the mid 1960s when Dale Fabrick and his helpers rotovated the entire course, removing some rocks and burying others. A start was made on the irrigation system.

In **1970-1989** a new clubhouse is built on the corner of the Crescent and Memorial in 1970. The course now shows two par threes at the start. (The second of these is now the chipping green and was formerly called "The Punch Bowl." Major reconfiguration of the greens took place and bunkers are now added.

In the **1989-2007** map the Punch Bowl is no longer used for play and, in order to make room for a new clubhouse in that location, the gulley hole is built in 1991.

In **2007-2013** the new clubhouse opens in 2008 and the course starts on a par five.

PERSONALITIES | 69

Some Art Bridge quotes:

> *I love the game. It's got me, body and soul, captivated. I love the challenge. I love the sociability. I love to meet and play with different people. I love to play different courses. I like green grass. It's just such a pleasant way of life.*

> *I wasn't a long hitter. I could get 250 yards without any trouble.*

> *I'm just a bum putter.*

> *I never met a golfer I didn't like.*

> *When you win you feel so good – on top of the world. When you lose, you can get depressed.*

Art Bridge, 1995

Art hit his first golf ball at age five – in the late 1920s. He lived beside a golf course but the owners didn't allow him to play there. He and his friends had no money and therefore no clubs. So they made their own. To do this they lit a bonfire out in a field and heated a piece of pipe red hot, bent it, flattened it on one side with a hammer and stuck a broom handle in it. Art played with homemade clubs until he was eight years old.

"I got my first real golf club then. It was a wooden shafted two iron. The hickory shaft was cut off so it would fit me. It was my pride and joy for years and years. Eventually, I broke the shaft."

Many years later (1971) he and his family moved to Qualicum Beach where his wife Maureen took up the game and progressed to a 15 handicap. The Bridges experienced a banner year in 1972. Art won the Men's Club Championship, Maureen, the Ladies' Club Championship and their youngest son, Kiernan the Junior Championship.

Art was the President of the club during the transition years when the town bought the golf course from the Brown family.

Maureen won the Ladies' Title six times, and Art the Men's Title six times.

His most memorable shot came in 1984 on the old number seven green. He scored an Albatross double eagle from the present number five tee when his second shot found the cup. Yardage 479. (This was before the gulley hole was built.)

Six Holes in one:
- 2 at Gorge Vale
- 3 at Qualicum Beach
- 1 at March Meadows

Lowest scores:
- 18 holes at Qualicum Beach – 64
- 9 holes at Qualicum Beach – 31

Jack Parker

Qualicum Beach residents driving out to the airport will see Bennett Road nearby. Jack was born there and the adjacent Parker Road was named after his family. The middle son of Fred and Ann Parker, Jack was born in 1934, his brother Fred arrived first in 1931 and latecomer Bert in 1940.

At age ten, Jack remembers that the clubhouse, pro shop and Qualicum Beach Resort Hotel were all located in the general area of what is now the third tee box. Young Jack spent a lot of time caddying for the professional of the day Dave MacLeod, a Scot from Aberdeen, the first fully qualified professional employed by the golf club.

By his own evaluation, Jack had his best years as a golfer between 1983 and 1988. In that period, he won the Men's Championship at Qualicum Beach four times. In 1987, he won the Qualicum Beach Championship, the May 24th Amateur and the Labour Day Tournament. "A hole in one is good fortune and good luck," says Jack. He has had five; four at Qualicum Beach and one at Eaglecrest.

Lowest scores:
- 18 holes at Qualicum Beach – 65
- 9 holes at Qualicum Beach – 30
- 18 holes at Eaglecrest – 69

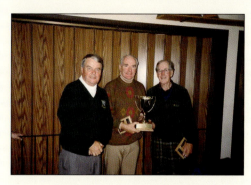

Club Trophy Winners 1993. Left to right – Claud Buchanan, Rob Hughes, and Bob Alford.

Bob Mitchell (left) and Jim Say were the first to run a tournament at QBMGC with the use of a computer in 1994 at the May 24th Men's Amateur. They usually played together sporting "plus fours" and natty white caps!

Three Stalwarts – 30 - year club members! Left to right: Ray Elder, Tats Aoki, and Bill Fayter.

23rd Annual Qualicum Foods Senior Ladies' Amateur

23rd Annual Qualicum Foods Senior Ladies' Amateur held August 5, 2011. 66 ladies entered this year's event. Deb Hutchinson of Storey Creek Golf Club captured the winning trophy in a sudden death play off with Billie Chang of Mount Brenton Golf Course.

Back row, left to right – Helen Williams, Sandi Reed, Pat Chern, Faith Kitzler, Charlotte Dunwoody, Irene Robson.   Middle row, left to right – Lynn Buchanan, Shirley Anderson, Jill Green. Front row – Angie Goodman, Joan Jeffs, Dea Kern, Ann LaJoie.

A Very Special Foursome

When this photograph was taken in 1995 Ray was 82, Buz 85, Dick 76 and George 84 years of age.

None of them did reach a hundred and five, but during their lifetimes, they typified all that is best about Qualicum Beach Memorial Golf Course. They played golf together as early as possible, every playable day. And loved it.

Left to right – Ray Zoost, Buz Broatch, Dick Bailey, George Hollins.

Part of their theme song:

"*And if you should survive to a hundred and five*

Look at all you'll derive just from being alive,

And here is the best part You'll have a head start

If you are among the very young at heart!"

Parker Family Photos, January 2004

Course was closed for 23 days due to heavy snow.

Howard has his sporting priorities straight

- an edited version of a newspaper article written by James Deacon for a local newspaper in 1983. Thanks to Gloria Miller, a long time member of the Qualicum Beach Golf Club, for providing the original article complete with a photo of "Howard the Duck", a mallard who spent his years generally enjoying life in and around the pond on what is now the eighth fairway. Howard was an unabashed freeloader who would happily avail himself of all that the passing golfers had to offer. He may well have done this for a decade. Howard passed away in 1983 or thereabouts - when once again his picture appeared in the local newspaper under the caption "Twas a sad day ... last week when Howard the resident philosopher at Qualicum Beach Memorial Golf Club, passed away. There will be no wake because Howard didn't like rough water."

There's a saying in one of the Eastern philosophies that you learn as much watching the river flow by as you do travelling up and down its length. With that in mind I decided to go have a visit with Howard.

Howard pretty much falls into the category of one who watches the river flow by. The only difference is that Howard spends his days on the golf course watching the golfers go by. He's there with the early-risers with dew on their heels, and he's there after the sun sets on the last foursome of the day.

You'd think all that golf watching would drive a guy to take up the game, but not Howard. He's smart enough to know he can do without the frustration, the lost balls and the green fees, and he also knows that if he stays put the people who feed him know where to find him.

So anyway, my purpose in siting down with old Howard for a chat was to sort out some of the raging sports issues of the day. It stood to reason that by watching the world go by, Howard might have attained wisdom beyond his stature.

Howard was unruffled as the questions overflowed in the early part of our conversation. Would Gretsky take on the rest of the league single-handed and outscore them all? Will Springwood Park ever be finished?

In his usual unflappable way Howard ignored my ranting and soon it was clear to me that I wasn't going to find answers to any of these burning questions if I didn't get a hold of myself.

Howard left me on my own to calm down and set out some priorities. Why get upset about Gretsky anyway?

Springwood is another one that can stand more time on the back burner; the all-round recreation park is still thousands of dollars and months of negotiations away from completion. It doesn't take a genius to figure that if it took years to get two baseball infields ready, finishing off the outfields and the soccer fields could be a project for future generations.

It was in a much clearer frame of mind that I left Howard. Out there on the ninth hole, where a water hazard acts as both home to Howard and magnet to errant drives, the world began to unfold as it should, or at least how it was going to whether we like it or not.

Yes, it had been an enlightening, if one-sided, conversation. Howard hadn't uttered a word the whole time. Howard is the consummate listener, a bartender serving piece of mind on the rocks who'll listen to anyone who brings him sunflower seeds or old bread to eat.

You see, Howard is a duck. A mallard, to be exact. Something happened to one of his wings, so he had the good sense to hang out in a place away from hungry eagles, but close to a steady food supply.

Smart guy that Howard.

james deacon

The Playing Professionals

James Arthur Montgomerie

James Montgomerie (Monty)

James was born in Port Elizabeth, South Africa in 1881. He attended elementary school in South Africa, then High School in Chelsea, England. He returned to South Africa to play rugby for the renowned Springboks and was known as "Monty the Fullback." He enlisted in the army and was commissioned as an officer during World War 1.

James moved to Canada where he met and married Gertrude Alice Martin. Gertrude died shortly after their son was born. James returned to South Africa leaving the child in the care of his sister-in-law in Victoria, B.C. He returned to Victoria in 1920 to retrieve his son, but his relatives would not give up the boy they had raised.

Monty returned once more to South Africa hoping to find employment in the diamond industry, but with limited success. His final trip to Canada came in 1932 when he moved to Qualicum Beach and worked at the Hotel and Golf Resort Course as a golf professional where he was known as 'Monty." He died in 1976 at the age of 95. His hobbies were rugby, soccer, golf, cricket and snooker. He loved spaniels.

Author: Garth Montgomerie (Grandson)

Dave MacLeod

Until April 1945, there was no playing professional at Qualicum Beach. The head Greenskeeper played that dual role. However in 1945, Qualicum was most fortunate in finding the services of Dave MacLeod, one of the leading teaching and professional golfers in B.C. who had training in Aberdeen, Scotland. Many demands were made on Dave's time and consequently he was asked to give lessons in practically all the golf centres in the Upper Island.

However, he took such a close interest in bringing the local links to a high degree of excellence that he was rarely able to get away from his club duties. Clearly, Dave loved the area around here so much that he, who once visited Vancouver on a regular basis, seldom went there any more.

In 1945, the club had a membership of 80 with Frank O. White as its President. Mr. White had previously been a member at Burquitlam, Point Grey and Marine Drive Golf Clubs in Vancouver.

The 1946 revival of the Upper Island Amateur was successfully staged on May 24th, 25th and 26th. Mr. M.B. Meredith of Vancouver was the winner of the Men's Championship and Mrs. F.J. Eves of Victoria won the Ladies' event.

It is worth remembering that, up until this date in 1946, seven Governors General of Canada had visited Qualicum Beach during their terms of office.

1946 Officers: President – Frank O. White; Vice-President – E. Leonard Boultbee; Secretary – George Walker.

Directors: F.C. Sweet; A.M. Johnstone; Professional: Dave Macleod.

On June 7, 1947 The Parksville /Qualicum Beach Progress reported...

"COAST GOLFDOM MOURNS PASSING OF DAVE MacLEOD"

West Coast golf suffered a grievous loss Wednesday as Dave MacLeod, an 'old school' professional who became one of the pioneers of the game in BC passed away suddenly at his home in Qualicum Beach.

Dave was appointed professional at the Qualicum Beach Club in 1945. And prior to that was the professional at Vancouver's Quilchena Golf Club and a skilled club maker for a commercial firm. He came to Vancouver in 1912 and was a resident of the West Coast ever after.

Archie Selwood, long time member and former President says; "Dave always brought great dignity to the first tee. He was a thorough gentleman and a strict disciplinarian who insisted upon full obedience to all the rules, etiquette and courtesies of golf. He was tremendously admired and will be sadly missed by us all."

Dave MacLeod is interred in Qualicum Beach Cemetery.

Dave MacLeod – second from right.

Jon Leyne

My family moved to Qualicum Beach in 1964 and soon after my father was hired as the club pro. It was one of the best things to ever happen to me. I was blessed to grow up in such a lovely spot – and to enjoy free golf throughout my childhood was a bonus.

My father had retired from the air force in Winnipeg a few years earlier. We moved to Vancouver Island immediately thereafter. He sold ads for the Nanaimo newspaper for a while, but when the golf pro position opened up, it was the dream job for him.

My first memory of the club is toting a junior set of clubs in a cheap purple carry bag around and around the course that first summer. I think my record was something like five rounds in a day.

The pro shop when Dad started was a little cottage on the grounds of the now long-gone Qualicum Beach Hotel. It was adjacent to an old clubhouse, just across Crescent Avenue from what is now the 3rd tee. A bit later they built a tiny little pro shop on the golf course itself, right behind what is now the 3rd tee. Later, they built a much bigger clubhouse and pro shop at the corner of Crescent and Memorial. The other significant project on the golf course during my childhood was a major upgrade in the late 1960s. The course was shut down for a long time as a beautification program took shape. Dozens of trees were planted, tons of rocks were picked and the entire course was plowed and re-seeded. I remember it was a community effort in which all sorts of people pitched in. My Boy Scout troop did its fair share of rock picking. An important personal measure of the passing years for me is the size of the trees that dot the course. They were two or three feet high when I helped plant some of them. I loved helping out around the course. I got to test-drive a riding mower one summer and specialized in the aprons around the greens. I was also the first sprinkler boy – although I preferred "senior irrigation technician" – when the new system got up and running. I moved sprinkler heads around the course once or twice a day, according to a colour-coded chart, for $40 a month. I drove an old brown golf cart that the course nursed along for years. It must have had 100,000 miles on it before it really packed it in. A memory flashes up as I write this – riding in a red Ford pickup at the crack of dawn with 100 feet of garden hose tied to the back, as Dad drove around and around each green to knock the dew off before the course opened for play. I guess we could have just got out and dragged it over the green by hand, but it was easier our way.

My father seemed to have a good relationship with most of the golfers. He was part of a core group that kept an endless gin rummy game – specifically called Nanaimo Rummy – running for years on end. A rotating band of members would sit in the clubhouse during the slow winter months and play for a penny a point, with remarkable intensity. The curses and insults would mount as they chased the same four or five dollars around for hours on end.

One specific memory – my father stuffed 20 pounds of rocks in the bottom of the bag of one of the summer regulars from Vancouver. He let him tote the rocks around for the duration of his summer stay, and then revealed the prank after the golfer's last inordinately tiring round of the summer.

My father had an Irish temper that would blow up on occasion. After a long day, an overly demanding golfer would occasionally push his button and he would go off like a rocket. A driver on Memorial Avenue once honked in the middle of his swing. Dad sent a mid-iron helicoptering over the road at the car, but missed. The few tantrums would end as quickly as they erupted. He loved the job. During the summer season, he worked from 6 am until dark every day of the week.

He was a fairly low handicapper when he started, around 6, which I believe was a prerequisite for the job. There's an old family photo album that shows him winning golf trophies in Dawson Creek, where he lived in earlier days. But he never had a lot of time to play in Qualicum, so I think his game suffered. Being a club pro is about the worst thing that can happen to your game.

My father was notorious with the kids of Qualicum Beach for how he conducted the golf ball trade. He had a monopoly on the retail market and abused his power mercilessly. Kids would find Titleists in perfect condition and bring them in to the pro shop in hopes of making 50 cents, before heading to the candy store. He would offer a dime or a quarter, tops. And anyone who tried to shortcut 'The Man' and sell directly to the golfers would be run off the course. Once a day or so he'd jump in a cart and whip around the course to terrify junior black market entrepreneurs, laughing his head off upon his return.

My connection in the pro shop landed me a gig caddying for Bob Hope a couple of times as a kid, which conferred celebrity status for a day or so at school.

My father worked for Alex Smith, who was the General Manager of the golf course and the Brown estate. He liked and respected him. But in the early 1970s there was some job consolidation at QB Memorial and my father found himself on a tractor, cutting fairways, which he didn't enjoy much, along with his pro shop duties. I believe Eaglecrest opened up in 1972 and the owners – Rafferty Chapman, John Boultbee, et al – successfully recruited him to move down the road and become pro there. He enjoyed himself there for several more years, gradually curtailing his work schedule. The management at Eaglecrest treated him very well, something I always appreciated. He was more or less fully retired by the early 1980s, and died suddenly of a heart attack on August 4, 1983, at the age of 70. Eaglecrest was good enough to put up a flagpole mounted in a stone cairn, with a plaque marking his contribution to golf in Qualicum Beach.

Author: Les Leyne (son),
March 17, 2011

Peter Nicholas Olynyk

Peter Nicholas Olynyk was born on September 23, 1915 in Nelson, B.C., the first of five children of immigrant parents William and Katherine. The Olynyk clan moved to Edmonton when Pete was just a child. As teenagers and young men, Pete and

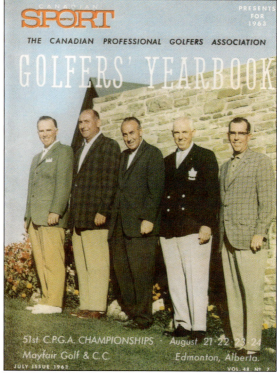

his younger brother Alex spent many years caddying and working at the Highlands Golf Course, and taking every opportunity to learn the art of golf. Alex became a professional golfer in 1940, Pete followed in 1944, at age 29. During the war years, Alex joined the infantry, serving in Europe; while Pete trained in sheet metal work, fabricating durable metal buildings for troops and equipment. After the war, Pete married Lucy Grace Muir and became assistant pro at the prestigious Mayfair Golf Club. After his promotion to head pro, his duties included operation of the pro shop, teaching golf lessons, and operating the driving range. Despite limited golf playing time, Pete did manage to win the Alberta Open Golf Tournament and finished in the top three several times. Alex and Pete operated one of Alberta's first indoor golf schools during the winter months on Jasper Avenue. The brothers also operated an outdoor driving range on Grierson Hill.

In 1963, Pete and his family moved to Calgary to oversee the design and construction of the new Shaw Nee Slopes Golf Course, eventually becoming the head pro. Evenings in the Olynyk household were often spent counting and bagging tees for sale in the pro shop.

A visiting relative who had retired to Vancouver Island encouraged Pete to have a look, perhaps to invest and eventually retire there. After a few trips, Pete and Lucy were convinced. They purchased a small acreage in Parksville with the idea of some day retiring, opening a driving range and teaching golf. Pete and Lucy and the younger children moved to a house in Qualicum Beach in 1974. Soon thereafter, Pete got to know the management of the Qualicum Beach Memorial Golf Course and eventually was offered a position

as its first teaching golf professional, also managing the pro shop and driving range. He continued in this capacity for four years until diagnosed with lung cancer in 1978. Despite treatment, he succumbed to his disease a little over a year later on May 20, 1980 aged 64. The Peter Olynyk Memorial Trophy was awarded each year for a time afterwards to the best Junior Golfer at Qualicum Beach Memorial Golf Course.

Pete and Lucy are survived by their sons, Gerry, a veterinarian in Calgary; Harry, a geologist in Brentwood Bay; Peter, a forester in Nanaimo; and daughters, Kathy, a nurse/horticulturalist in Parksville; and Kelly, a writer in Qualicum Beach. There are also eight grandchildren.

Author: Gerry Olynyk (son),
March 13, 2011

Steve Cikaluk

When head Pro Steve Cikaluk of the Glendale Golf & Country Club in Winnipeg, Manitoba headed to the west coast in May of 1980 to accept a new job offer at Qualicum Beach Memorial Golf Course, Vancouver Island, he knew he would be wearing two hats – that as manager, overseeing all course operations, including food services – and as golf pro, providing lessons (seniors included), supporting charitable organizations, customizing and repairing clubs, and encouraging teens as well as younger children to take up the game. But for Steve, the biggest challenge of all would be to make a 9-hole "easy" course into the toughest "easy" course around. And the most beautiful and well groomed nine holes in Canada.

Cikaluk turned professional in 1956 working as assistant pro to the late Frank Willey at the Riverside Golf Course in Edmonton. From there Steve travelled to Winnipeg, where he worked as assistant pro to Chick Duncan at the Niakwa Country Club before moving on in 1964 to be head pro at the Elmhurst Golf and Country Club in the same city. During winter months Steve, a seasoned curling professional as well as golf pro, curled and taught that game as well.

In 1970, Steve became head Pro at Winnipeg's Glendale Golf & Country Club where he remained until the call to Vancouver Island came in 1980. With his wife Lilliane, and their children, Steve moved to Qualicum Beach, BC to take over a private golf course owned by former Home Oil president Bob Brown.

In 1981 the course changed hands and now became the property of Qualicum Beach. Not interested in running a golf course, the town turned this task over to the golf club with Cikaluk, an experienced and talented professional to redesign and manage the course. Steve went immediately to work assessing the course needs and urging the Club to approve the necessary changes. The course would soon become the town's greatest asset. Over the years seven of the nine greens were redesigned and rebuilt. Today there are 27 different tees, an automated sprinkling system throughout the course and an updated and improved clubhouse facility.

Management can promise that regardless of how much rain falls, the golf course can now boast of being the driest in the area. As for the Town of Qualicum Beach, the Town fathers couldn't be happier. Their shrewd investment has proven to be one of their best assets in tourism and community popularity. Where else do you find a beautiful golf course situated in the middle of town? Even celebrities like the late Bob Hope and the late Bing Crosby have dropped anchor here to play a round of golf.

(Excerpts from an article by Shirley Elliot written for the Nisku Wildcatter (an Alberta Newspaper) April 1998. Shirley Elliott was President of Qualicum Beach Memorial Golf Club during the years 1996 – 1998; she also won the Ladies' 18-hole Championship in 1999.)

The Present

History of our golf club "Q" Logo

The present logo was created in 2004 incorporating the following ideas which were submitted by the members of the time —

- the (then) second green (now the first green)
- the Straight of Georgia
- Chrome Island
- Mount Arrowsmith
- a golf ball
- a golf club
- the eagle tree

and many more ideas …

We took the list of ideas to a creative Partisan Graphic Artist, Jean-Claude, Marketing Dynamics Intrinsic Communication Solutions Ltd., then located in Chilham Village, in Qualicum Beach, who, after several drafts, critiqued by the members, created our present logo.

- The "circle" – is the green and the golf ball
- The long blue "tail" is the Straight of Georgia
- The green "hump" is Mount Arrowsmith, and
- The small green "swoop" is Chrome Island.

86 | THE PRESENT

THE PRESENT | 87

EDITOR@PQBNEWS.COM

New golf clubhouse opens in QB

Grand opening

By FRED DAVIES
News Reporter

It's a fancy new facility already receiving rave reviews from golfers and on Saturday the new clubhouse at Qualicum Beach Memorial Golf Course held it's official grand opening.

Mayor Teunis Westbroek, before a small gathering outside, handed out lifetime memberships to members of the Brown family — property owners and instrumental, Westbroek said, in making the building's completion reality.

"This is a first class, beautiful, facility second to none on the Island," he said just prior to cutting the red ribbon that made it all official.

The mayor noted the project had all the appearances of an economic success as well and said the first payment of $50,000 towards a loan from the town was delivered recently months prior to his expectation.

reporter@pqbnews.com

qualicum beach
GRAND OPENING

THE NEW CLUBHOUSE at the Qualicum Beach Memorial Gold Course is now officially open. Mayor Teunis Westbroek cut the ribbon on the weekend, alongside club president George Mooney. For more, see page B6.

business
OPENING DAY

MAYOR TEUNIS WESTBROEK greets visitors on their way into the new clubhouse at Qualicum Beach Memorial Golf Course Saturday during grand opening celebrations.

LOCAL RULES

- Please keep power and pull carts 30 feet from tees and greens.
- Maximum - 4 players per group.
- Fairway Markers - free relief from marker for swing - stance and line.
- R.C.G.A. rules of golf govern play.
- Out of bounds is indicated by white stakes on holes 1, 3, 4, 6, 7, 8 and 9.
- Lateral water hazard indicated by red stakes on holes 4 and 7.
- Water hazard indicated by yellow stakes on hole 8.

GOLFERS ARE RESPONSIBLE FOR ALL BALLS HIT OFF PROPERTY

469 Memorial Avenue
Qualicum Beach, BC
Canada V9K 1G8

Proshop: 250.752.6312 • Fax: 250.752.6550
proshopqbmgc@shaw.ca • www.golfqualicum.ca

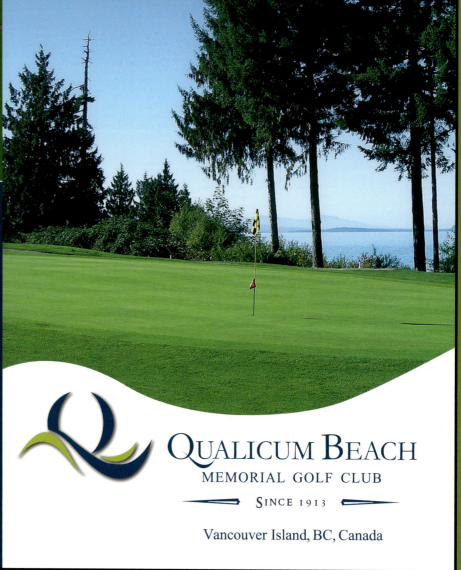

QUALICUM BEACH
MEMORIAL GOLF CLUB
SINCE 1913

Vancouver Island, BC, Canada

Hole	Slope / Rating	1	2	3	4	5	6	7	8	9	Out	Init	1	2	3	4	5	6	7	8	9	In	Total
Blue	M: 113 / 66.8 L: 129 / 73.0	510	225	325	300	143	400	462	335	144	2844		510	225	325	300	143	400	462	335	144	2844	5688
White	M: 113 / 65.2 L: 122 / 70.6	480	195	300	285	118	377	450	315	135	2655		480	195	300	285	118	377	450	315	135	2655	5310
Red	M: 102 / 62.8 L: 114 / 67.6	460	175	280	275	100	345	427	235	126	2423		460	175	280	275	100	345	427	235	126	2423	4846
																						Hcp	Net
Par		5	3	4	4	3	4	5	4	3	35		5	3	4	4	3	4	5	4	3	35	70
+/-																							
Men's Handicap		1	5	11	9	17	3	7	13	15			2	6	12	10	18	4	8	14	16		
Ladies' Handicap		1	15	9	3	11	5	7	13	17			2	16	10	4	12	6	8	14	18		

Pin Position on Green: Front, Middle, Back

Fairway Markers: 100 yds, 150 yds, 200 yds

PGA BRITISH COLUMBIA

Instruction Available

Player:
Attest:
Date:

Coastal Colour Printing 79082/09

Our Clubhouse Today

During the late 1990s, it was becoming apparent that the old Qualicum Beach Memorial Golf Course clubhouse, situated on the corner of Crescent and Memorial, was becoming dilapidated and difficult to maintain. With the transition of the golf club administration to the annually-elected Executive Board of Directors, it appeared to be the right time to commence planning a new clubhouse. It was decided that the new building should not only be functional, but should also enhance the idyllic and beautifully presented golf course. Thus the siting on the present area was chosen and discussions between the representatives of the Town Council (the landlords) and select committees from the golf club executive board and club members commenced. Presentations of various designs were considered, each with advantages. However, a design which featured amenities for the club members, a golf pro shop, easy access to adequate car parking and restaurant facilities became paramount. Running parallel with the subject of design of the building were the proposals for financing the project. In late 2006, the Town Council agreed to finance the balance of the project over a 25-year term repayable by the golf club membership. Working with a Vancouver-based architect, Jerry Doll of Neale Staniskis Doll & Adams, the design was discussed and it was agreed that the concept should be a "West Coast" style building. As plans were being finalized and the initial soil testing began, it was quickly realized that the planned site was on a First Nations midden and burial site. With the cooperation of the federal and local authorities, Qualicum First Nations Band and the incumbent golf club administration, an archaeological dig began in January 2007 lasting for a three-month period. As a result of the dig, the clubhouse site was moved towards Memorial Avenue to respect the environment without reducing the panoramic views from the second floor of the proposed clubhouse. Windley Contracting Ltd., under the watchful eye of Project Manager, Mark Brown and Construction Manager, Walter Hoogland, began the groundwork in April 2007 for the construction of the 9,200 square foot clubhouse. The building was completed in January 2008.

The official grand opening took place May 3, 2008. Whilst the clubhouse has undergone minor internal changes to facilitate the ongoing popularity and success of the restaurant and pro shop facilities, it is generally felt by the membership and visitors alike that the combination of the new clubhouse and the golf course provide a near perfect environment to play golf and socialize.

Author: Leonard Lloyd
November 2011

Ross Mantell

Tall, with an easy going manner, a ready smile and an infectious chuckle, Ross Mantell is a natural fit for a golf club that includes many retirees and a sprinkling of younger members.

He was born and raised in Victoria (Gordon Head), attended Cedar Hill Junior High School and graduated from Mount Douglas Senior High School in 1988. His first golf club job was cleaning clubs at Uplands Golf Club. He went to Ventura College just north of Los Angeles under golf coach Brian Marshall. After earning his degree in Physical Education, there followed a stay at Cal State University at San Bernadino, a Division 2 NCAA School.

Ross played on the golf team there and experienced the thrill of actually flying to golf tournaments. In 1994, he came home and, through the back door, qualified for the Provincial Amateur Tournament; he finished fifth and qualified for the Provincial Willingdon Cup Team.

When an offer came up to become assistant professional at Royal Colwood, he headed off for more schooling to become a full club professional. He completed his qualifications at Camosun College. December 2003 saw the posting for the Head Professional's job at Qualicum Beach. Jim Goddard, his boss at Cordova Bay, encouraged Ross to apply. Ross did apply, and he was hired to begin his new job as Head Professional at Qualicum Beach Memorial Golf Club on March 23, 2004.

Ross is married to Janet, and together they have a daughter Elise, and a son, Parker.

Ross and his well-qualified staff – Tyson Lemon, Steven MacPherson and Matt Cella – always seem to remember everyone's name. Ross and Steven teach us how to improve our game, they organize hundreds of tee times and tournament schedules with what appears to be very little effort and they are always smiling!

Left to right – Ross Mantell, Tyson Lemon, Matt Cella, Steven MacPherson.

Pro Shop.

Thalassa Restaurant

On Monday March 16, 2009, a new relationship starts and an ever-expanding family is created. Thalassa (meaning "Ocean" in Greek) Restaurant is the culmination of two families, four children and a future that continues to bless us with much joy, awards, gratification and community support that continues to create, without a doubt, memories that will last forever.

On a snowy day in February 2009, the listing in the Nanaimo Bulletin read, "New restaurant for lease, on a golf course, fully furnished, restaurant managers needed. For details, please call Mr. Harry Adshead or Mr. Don Reid." The next few weeks played out like a movie … a quick phone call, a lunch meeting at the golf club the next day, a family meeting, Harry and Don having lunch in Ladysmith "just in the neighbourhood" they said, and the so-called Greek Mafia breakfast two weeks later and the deal was done. The rest as it's said … is history.

Left to right – Petros, Kalli, Oura, Kymon.

While Oura Giakoumakis and Kalli Bourodemos are working the front of the restaurant welcoming their patrons, their husbands Kymon and Petros are busily running the kitchen and "mastering the children's schedules."

Thalassa's first month of operation was nothing short of amazing for our two families, but it also came with sadness at the loss of our Yiayia Kalliopi, her portrait graces our bar front as she watches over us. The driving forces of our beliefs are – dedication to family, to the golf club members, and to our community.

2011 brought some amazing recognition to Thalassa Restaurant; we were overjoyed and honoured to accept the "Best New Business" award; and to the people of Qualicum Beach, we thank you for choosing our "Chili"; we are very happy you enjoy it!

To our new family and our staff, to the associates we work with, the grounds crew and club members, and to all the folks who drop by our restaurant, we wholeheartedly thank you all for the memories and for allowing us to be part of your lives.

Authors: Oura, Kalli, Kymon and Petros

Rory Johnstone

Our Greens' Superintendent

"My favourite time of day is five in the morning when the sun comes up; when the golf course is in its prime state. Our profession is a real connection with Nature, watching things grow and the pleasure that you see people taking from what they experience here. People give the ground's crew genuine compliments.

We are really the stewards of the property and the land. We are environmentalists. We don't like chemicals – they are a last resort. Our crew is long-term with excellent work ethics. The guys enjoy what they do and the club has treated them well."

Rory's golf course experience began in 1979 at Eaglecrest when the second nine holes were being built there. (He actually began playing golf at age twelve). He had been there for two years when an opening occurred at Qualicum Beach. The Manager, Alex Smith, offered Rory the job of Greens' Superintendent after he had spent a summer acclimatizing. Rory accepted the position.

At the outset of his tenure, the land was the same as it had been for many years, but compared to the present, everything else was quite different. The greens were quite small; irrigation was minimal, as was maintenance, and the tee boxes, too, were not of the

Back row, left to right – Rob Liefer, Ed Rochon, Chris Hood
Front row, left to right – Rory Johnstone, Zack Owen.

required size. The watering system was called valve and key which meant that the sprinkling valves had to be moved by hand and rotated. The clubhouse, which stood at the corner of Memorial and Crescent, was built by Pat Gadd Construction in 1970.

When the town bought the golf course from the Brown family, the first Pro/Manager, Steve Cikaluk was hired and long-term planning began. The initial aim was to get all the tees and greens built up and irrigated. The plan was to expand the greens in the range of 3,000 to 5200 square feet apiece, which would enable them to handle the foot traffic of sixty-five to seventy-eight thousand rounds of golf per year. Much of this was accomplished.

The gulley hole was built so that we could discontinue using the old number two green – the one that is now used for chipping practice just below the putting green. It was called the Punch Bowl. That was done to provide space for the building of the new clubhouse which we opened in 2008.

The overall plan for the new layout design was produced by Warren Radomsky Golf Limited of Lumsden, Saskatchewan. At this time it was also decided to install logs along Crescent Road to stop drivers from vandalizing the fairways and greens with their cars.

Two greens were rebuilt every second year over a five-year period. All of the greens except the present number three are new. The sodding for all of this work was done by our own crew from our own ' nursery ' on the grounds.

The golf course equipment is purchased when needed – not leased.

"I remember when I was very young, Lesley Smith's Dad (Alex) called and said we needed three caddies because Bob Hope was coming. I got to the course and there were ten or twenty people standing by the tee. When Mr. Hope arrived there were two hundred. He signed every autograph given to him. He was just so easy with people. He talked all the time, telling stories."

THE PRESENT | 99

David Green

Guardian of the Keep – Qualicum Beach Memorial Golf Club celebrates its 100th anniversary in 2013. I have the good fortune to share in this history since becoming part-time bookkeeper in 2004. The position provided an opportunity to apply my accounting skills and develop my golf game. Little did I realize that the club, its members, boards and patrons would provide my social network in the Qualicum Beach Memorial Family!

My position provides assistance to members and the board with projects and concerns that arise while providing a liaison for issues that develop. The club has remained a close family through its history, providing the organization for golf but also a support network through life's challenges and a social outlet for celebration and friendship. New arrivals are welcomed into our membership fostering the continual evolution and change that is so critical for a strong and vibrant golf club.

This process has been especially invigorating over recent years gathering information on the club history, watching past and present members discussing changes that have occurred and memories that have been forged since the beginning. Being a part of this process has been an honour and a privilege one does not take lightly.

Author: David Green

The Ladies' Division

We are extremely indebted to Blanche Barrett, who in 1991 as Ladies' Captain, directed some members to gather all the old minutes (some very sketchy) and write a history of the Ladies' Club. Acknowledgments and appreciation go to Arlene Lamont, Pat Mackie and "fellow club members" as well as Mary Bullock who kept all the snapshots.

The following is an abridgment of that history.

No record can be located for the first nine years of this club's existence, unfortunately, although we have found a list of trophy winners for 1955. Minutes of a 1956 meeting indicate it to be "the 9th annual meeting with eleven members in attendance," so we conclude that a ladies' club was established in 1947. Indeed, we have a copy of an Application for Membership in the Canadian Ladies' Golf Union, dated October 14, 1947.

No official record is available listing the Charter Members; however, the following names have been suggested by longstanding members' best recollection:

Mary Money, Muriel Corfield, Edna Dougan, Molly Whitmee, Grace Campbell, Edna Kinkade, Edie Beaton, Ruby Crawley, Jeanette Forrester, Locky Montgomery, Ann Parker, Mae Paterson.

Between 1956 and 1968, there appears to have been a twelve-year struggle to sustain the very existence of a ladies' club in Qualicum Beach. Memberships fluctuated between only seven to fifteen ladies, despite the efforts of Dave McLeod, acting pro/manager, who offered lessons at no charge to interested ladies. Eventually, in the Spring of 1969, the club temporarily disbanded for lack of active participants. Eight ladies revived the club that same fall, four of whom were new members. It is interesting to note that 1964 marks the first time that members are being referred to on a first name basis in the minutes, rather than "Mrs. Fred Doe," etc. although the group is still a relatively small one.

Ladies' Day Golf, initially held on Thursdays, was changed in 1964 to Mondays. This was done to accommodate members who worked in local stores and businesses that closed on Mondays. Playing times were split, with a 10:30 a.m. and a 6:30 p.m. starting time. Wednesday became Ladies' Day in 1970 and ten o'clock was the tee off time. By July, increasing membership numbers necessitated an "early" starting time of nine o'clock!

The following excerpts highlight some of the changes over the years:

1973: A set of bylaws was adopted by the now forty-member club and more emphasis was being placed on the finer points of the game. There was increasing interest in the official rules of golf, hence a Rules Committee was established and was a fixture sheet for the club.

1974: Ladies' Club fees rose from $7 to $10. Three new executive positions were created – Interclub, Rules, and Match Chairman.

1977: The course yardage was changed from 5086 yards to 5568 yards. This changed the course rating to 69. Social functions held in the clubhouse required a liquor permit (purchased for $2) so that beer ($.60 a glass) and hard liquor ($.75 an ounce) could be served on these occasions. Eventually, these liquor permits rose in price to $10, which caused enough controversy to become an item on the meeting agenda. Maureen Bridge had a hole-in-one at Port Alberni – she won a trailer and lost her amateur status for two years.

1978: Nanaimo held the Ladies' Annual Championships as it was the only 18-hole course in the district.

1982: Two distinct groups had evolved within the Ladies' Club of 82 members. Both shared Wednesday play competing separately as nine or eighteen-hole players. One nine-hole player would join three eighteen-hole players then drop off when the nine-hole game was completed. Green fees were $10 for 18 eighteen holes; $7 for nine holes.

1984: A year of change – clubhouse renovations were completed and a resident caterer was established – Halloween and Christmas parties initiated the new clubhouse – a new dishwasher was donated by the now over one hundred-member ladies' club – winners for the season were honoured at a fall wind-up party, a change from previous years when awards were a part of the annual banquet and dance – a separate nine-hole club championship was played – tee times were instituted on a trial basis – a preference for conventional golf took precedence over "fun/trick" type events on Ladies' day and – pre-registration for the weekly draw became necessary because of the number of participants.

1985: Interclub transportation fees were $3.50 to Comox and Sunnydale and $3.00 to Port Alberni and Nanaimo.

1989: The first Qualicum Beach Senior Ladies' Open Tournament was held on September 22nd, organized by Mary Bullock.

1990: Due to the large number of ladies wishing to join the Ladies' Clubs (an all-time high of 140), it was decided the nine and eighteen-hole clubs would be separated and each have their own executive and manage their own play. Both clubs continued to play on Wednesday as the Board did not approve allocating a second day for the ladies. However, instituting tee times on Wednesday starting with the nine hole club at 7:30 a.m. eliminated the slow play and helped clear the first tee for other members much earlier than the shotgun start method.

1991: All the members' names were entered into the computer and everyone was given their own secret code word so no one else (except authorized persons) could make any changes to their records.

Disbursed throughout the numerous years of minutes, the name Barbara Robinson kept popping up. The 1991 summary ends with a heartfelt thanks to Barb for all her work, especially her many floral arrangements over the years.

The Present:

The nine and eighteen-hole clubs continue to play on Wednesday as begun in 1991, although they now alternate taking early and late tee times on a monthly basis. In 2011, we have fifty-five members in the Eighteen-hole club, and 44 members in the Nine-hole club. Tee times and other important notices are usually communicated through email.

The ladies compete in a provincial Pin Round once a month. As well as our club championships, we have several other club competitions including the Money Memorial, Fred Sweet and Tulip Trophy. Our members enjoy playing in the Zone 6 tournaments as well as Team Play and Senior Buttons. Recently, informal interclubs have been popular as well.

The Qualicum Beach Senior Ladies' Open has been very successful every August. This is organized by a separate committee and supported by our members with assistance from the Men's Club and our professionals.

One of our club positions is that of Historian. Over the years, several albums have been stuffed with photos and news clippings of our various activities. They reveal more than words ever could, the many happy times and abiding friendships that have been forged at Qualicum Beach Memorial Golf Club.

Author: Lynn Buchanan

The Men's Division

Two World Wars severely hampered the growth and development of the male membership in the club. It is not recorded what the actual population of the village amounted to during the years 1914 – 18 but it was certainly in the hundreds and not thousands. Also, those who played here were mostly the guests of General Money and not casual drop ins. Money's guests came largely from Victoria and getting here was a major trip on the newly constructed railway or by automobile over roads that were a far cry from what we use today. The local men worked in the three local sawmills and had neither the time nor the money to participate in this relatively new local sport. (Our course is the fourth oldest in the Province).

We know that the population of the village shortly after incorporation in 1943 was 304. It is fair to suggest that the male population at the height of World War II was not large. Some local men did not return from the conflict. A graph of population growth shows very little change until 1951 when it doubled and reached 771. Perhaps the arrival of Dave MacLeod from Aberdeen, Scotland, in 1947 to become the first qualified playing professional might have signified an upturn in Men's Club members. Even in 1980, when the town bought the golf course from the Brown Family, the population had not yet reached 3,000.

In recent times, the Men's Club has met on Sunday mornings – Men's Day – and holds club competitions. Handicaps are used most of the time. Trophies are awarded at the end of each season and some bear the names of golfers and companies who have contributed much to the club: F.O. White, Art Higgs, Art Chapman, Jamieson Trophy, Manulife and Mertz Haden are the major ones. Art Higgs also looked after the trout hatchery which was located in the creek at the bottom of the gulley. In this year of 2011, a Nine-Hole Division of the Men's Club was established and shares the tee times with the Eighteen-Hole Club.

The Men's Club relinquished the running of the May 24th Qualicum Beach Men's Amateur Tournament in 2003. At this time, a club member, Doug McAree, volunteered to form a committee to run the event. The Quality Foods Men's Amateur Committee is currently headed by Bob Smillie. The best golfers in this part of Vancouver Island are attracted to what is one of the first major tournaments of the season and prizes are substantial.

Computers were first used by the late Bob Mitchell in the 1993 event to assist in, and speed up, the scoring tabulation. Prior to that, scores were recorded by hand on large score sheets taped to the windows and notice boards outside the clubhouse. It is fair to say that this was a laborious process. Today it is hard to imagine a tournament being run without a computer.

As of 2010, the Men's Club is operated by committee. In this year of 2011, the committee is comprised of the following members: Captain – Bob Benning; Vice-Captain – Don Reid; Draw Master – Jim Reynolds; Treasurer – Jim Horn; Draw Team Members – Phil Hedderly, Eduardo De Cairos, Peter Drummond, and Jerry Reed. This formatting has proved to be very successful and will probably be continued.

THE PRESENT

THE PRESENT | 121

THE PRESENT | 123

THE PRESENT | 125

THE PRESENT | 129

THE PRESENT | 131

THE PRESENT | 133

THE PRESENT | 135

Rhyme Of The Ancient Golfer

As I walk those treasured fairways
Among my golfing peers,
I wonder how the course might look
In another hundred years.
Will the cedar trees we've planted here
Reach high into the sky,
And will the blossoms smell as sweet
When balmy breezes sigh?

Will eagles still be standing guard
High in the "Eagle Tree"?
Will seals and sea lions still exist
To bask there in the sea?
And what of the herd of tiny deer
In the gully off number five?
Will Mother Nature be kind to them
In their struggle to survive?

Will members still view from the tee
Mount Arrowsmith in awe,
Or watch the sunset on number one
And marvel at what they saw?
Will this playground still be fondly known
As "God's Own Waiting Room"
Where many a golfer in our day,
Have willed their ashes strewn?

Those of us who've loved this place,
And tended it with care,
Have gloried in the fellowship
And friendships nurtured here.
And though the skills deteriorate,
The drives not near as long,
You'll find us on the course each day,
Slowed down, but playing on.

So, when members of a future
Generation come to play,
When teeing off on number five,
At dawning of the day,
If you sense an unseen presence
Standing near you on the tee.
Or may hear the eerie echo
Of a golf ball off a tree.

If you hear the sound of softly padding
Footsteps in the dew.
Fear not, it's us, the ghosts
Of ancient golfers playing through.

© 2010 Gus Barrett

> "Those of us who've loved this place, and tended it with care, have gloried in the fellowship and friendships nurtured here."

Gus Barrett

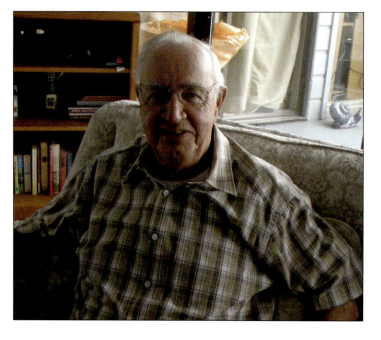

Gus was born in Bishop's Cove, Newfoundland, before it became a Province in 1949. He is, therefore, a "New Canadian." When Newfoundland became a province, Gus joined the RCMP and immediately asked for a Northern Service posting. His wish was granted and he found himself living in Whitehorse, Yukon Territory. There he met Blanche, a nurse and native of Dawson City. After their marriage, Gus transferred from the RCMP to Canada Customs.

The Barretts left the Yukon in 1967 and moved to Trail in the West Kootenays, the year that Nancy Greene from Rossland, BC, won her first of two World Cups in skiing. Gus and Blanche then spent five years in Quesnel, BC, (1968-73) and the final thirteen years of his working career in Port Alberni, BC.

Gus and Blanche have served as Captains of the Men's and Ladies' Clubs respectively and both have been members of the Board of Directors. Gus is the author of a delightful book called "Poetry and Other Nonsense" which he published in 2005.

AFTERWORD

So who are we who have chosen to make Qualicum Beach possibly the last stop on our journey through life and try to preserve some of the halcyon days of not too long ago?

We are here by choice. Often times our arrival was planned well ahead; others have come here by sheer chance. There are few, if any, who would change and go elsewhere, having sampled the lifestyle and climate in this hallowed place.

Describing the golfers of Qualicum Beach as a motley crew would be a good start. By definition, the word 'motley' means; a combination of diverse or clashing elements which fits us quite well. A cross section of our membership shows that virtually every profession and vocation is represented among us and there may be a few we haven't thought of.

Folks who have reached the very peak of their life pursuits come to Qualicum Beach and offer their services as volunteers. Therefore, when Boards of Directors, Committees and the like are formed, it is unlikely that there will be unanimity let alone conformity. "Been there, done that" is a common expression.

However, much thought goes into looking forward, often with great imagination and positive vision. A look at the maps in our book indicates how the golf course has been nurtured, protected and, to an extent, reinvented by a succession of owners, designers, greens' superintendents and playing professionals.

And that kind of care continues when we see that the last green to be rebuilt (the present number three) in the present era will have its location and contours changed very soon. Soon, too, we will see the new club flag flying proudly alongside that of the town and our great country. All three will greet the visitor driving into our parking lot. There will be a new and exciting appearance to the front of the clubhouse – different, elegant and memorable for future tourists and local residents alike.

The present playing professionals and their assistants are cast in the mold of the late Alex Smith who gave his all to this golf course for more than thirty years. The grounds' crew has the same dedication and passion that will keep these fairways green and immaculate for the foreseeable future.

That future will be assured if individuals of the present day continue to devote their lives to this heavenly place. The testing time will come when the Town of Qualicum Beach becomes –as it surely will – The City of Qualicum Beach. Thankfully we can rest content that these priceless lands cannot be used for any purpose other than a golf course or public park in perpetuity. There is a legal Covenant that was signed on August 31, 1981 guaranteeing this.

However, the course must continue to evolve as it has over the last twenty years in particular. It is constructed on one hundred feet of sand and so the percolation rate is higher than any other course on Vancouver Island. Tee boxes will be rebuilt, as will some greens. Trees will be blown down and replaced. The ladies' tee box in the gulley will have a reinforced embankment.

As long as nothing is allowed to stand still and stagnate, all will be well. And as we celebrate our first centennial with passion and gusto, our future seems assured.

SPECIAL THANKS

My sincere thanks to those who gave freely of their time and for sharing their memories – Roger Whitmee, Jack, Fred and Bert Parker, Bert and Grace Topliffe, Bob Bagnall, Pat Chern, Gerald and Verona Sharman, Fran Dobinson, Mikey Aylesworth, Kelly Olynyk, Terry Murray, Les Leyne, Barrie McWha, Michael Riste, John Watson, Viola Brown, Barb Penner, Susan Boyce, Bev Lasure, Sandi Reed, David Green, Brad and Hazel Wylie, George Mooney, Len Lloyd, Evelyn and Earle Mitchell, The Mants, Evelyn Miller, Grace Hall, Ross Mantell, Jean Smith, Leslie and Roger Williamson, Irene Robson, Garth Montgomery, Laurie Artiss, Eve Johnson.

Roger Whitmore and Jack Parker, for sharing their family photo collections; Grace Hall for her photo of Bob Hope; Bonnie Boyd for sharing Bob Hope's autograph; BC Golf House and Barry McWha for sharing their abundant golf archives and photos; and to the Qualicum Beach Museum and Archives, for sharing historic documents and photos.

Lois Brown, an accomplished professional photographer and daughter of Genevieve and R.A. Brown, for her many photographs of our beautiful golf course as it is today. Lois also wrote a compelling account of her parents' lives.

Teunis Westbroek, Mayor of Qualicum Beach, for his trust, support and encouragement in the writing of this book, and to staff of the Town of Qualicum Beach, with special thanks to Mark Brown, Trudy Coates, Heather Svensen, John Marsh and Luke Sales for their time, support, computer skills and help in researching historical data.

Jean Smith for her skilled reading and editing of the manuscript and providing her valuable insights.

Wendy Shaw for the inspirational leadership she gave as the Chair of the "100th Anniversary Steering Committee" and her determination to produce a first class coffee table book – there are not enough words to thank her. She was passionate about the book from day one. Thanks also to Ray Shaw for his quiet support.

My gratitude and love goes to my wife Lynn, without whose help, love, understanding and extraordinary patience, it would not have been possible for me to accomplish the writing of this book.

Left to right – Wendy Shaw, Lynn Buchanan.

BIBLIOGRAPHY

OLSON, Arv 1935 –

Backspin: 100 Years of Golf in British Columbia

WYLIE, Bradley C.

Qualicum Beach

A History of Vancouver Island's Best Kept Secrets

Hignall Printing Limited,

Winnipeg, Manitoba

RISTE, Michael

Just Call Me Mac, The Biography of Arthur Vernon Macan

Oscar's Press, Vancouver, BC

FOLK, Julie

Wascana at 100

First Printing 2011

Print West

Regina, SK

CPGA GOLF MAGAZINE

Zone 11

July 1947

Sun setting over the golf course bringing the promise of another day of golf in paradise!

Photograph by Wendy Shaw

Qualicum Beach Memorial Golf Club Junior Championship Donated by Peter Olynyk: 1976 Kim Collins 1977-1978 Paul Parker 1979 Richard Bridge 1980 Pat Collins 1981 Steve Watson 1982 Darryl Vossler 1983 Steve Watson 1984 Pat Collins 1985 Ryner Wilson 1986 Ryner Wilson 1987 Joff Filmer 1989 Kevin Cross 1991 Devon Peterson 1993 Kevin Mowatt 1995 Brook Kastelsky 1999-2000 Dave Duncan 2001-2002 Griffin Gilmore 2003 Andrew Locke 2004-2005-2006 Derek Spink 2007-2008 Joel Kumlin **Qualicum Beach Memorial Golf Club Art Chapman Memorial Trophy:** 1987 Art Bridge 1988 Jack Parker 1989 Ralph Baddeley 1990 Jim Wilson 1991 Jack Parker 1992 Blair Loggie 1993 Jim Wilson 1994 Roy Finck 1995 Jack Lasure 1996 Jack Parker 1997 Ajit Manhas 1998 Ted Powell 1999 Peter Phillippe 2000 Ernie Bentley 2001 Burke Bullock 2002 Ernie Bentley 2003 Bill Bennett 2004 Gross: Bill Bennett Net: Doug McAree 2005 Gross: Ken Vail Net: Jim Simpson 2006 Gross: Jim Paterson Net: George Ashcroft 2007 Gross: John McLennan Net: Jim Reynolds 2008 Gross: Roger Kaye Net: Ted Powell 2009 Mike Hayes 2010 Les Pockett 2011 **Qualicum Beach Memorial Golf Club Senior Ladies Quality Foods Amateur Open:** 1989 Betty Cone 1990 Yvonne Hall 1991 Margatet Thompson 1992 Joy Armstrong 1993-1994 Trudie Newman 1995 Maxine Danielson 1996 Trudi Newman 1997 Ida Wickham 1998 Frances Shaw 1999 Katy McCuish 2000 Mikey Aylesworth 2001 Joan Kossey 2002 Katy McCuish 2003 Doris Ellis 2005 Johnna Dodd 2006 Wendy MacKenzie 2007 Johnna Dodd 2008-2009-2010-2011 Deb Hutchinson **Qualicum Beach Memorial Golf Club Eagle Trophy Most Improved Player Ladies 9 Hole Division:** 1995-1996 Elaine Mooney 1997 Gerry Phillippe 1998 June Watson 1999 Jennie Mellis 2000 Meta van Pelt 2001-2002 June Dunn 2003 Joan Forgie 2004 Hilary Avis 2005 Muriel Bentley 2006 Gill Taylor 2007 Helena Maki 2008 Pat Rooke 2009 Donna Oodcock 2010 Bernice Sloper 2011 Sheila Kovach **Qualicum Beach Memorial Golf Club Junior Club Champion Under 14:** 1982-1983 David Newsted 1984 Joff Filmer 1985 Curtis Thompson 1986 Georald Ingborg 1987 Ryner Wilson 1989 Kevin Cross 1993 Darren Terhune 1999 Lee Crites 2000 Kevin Lemke 2001 Andrew Locke 2002-2003 Derek Spink **Qualicum Beach Memorial Golf Club Ladies Herbert Rose Bowl:** 1948-1949 L Good 1950 W A Paterson 1951 W Buckingham 1952 B Lowe 1953 G E H Montgomery 1954 R Forrester 1955 D Dougan 1956 W Shelly 1957 W A Paterson 1959 Mary Bullock 1964 E Hobson 1970 Molly Snow 1971 Frances Wilson 1972 Laila Raynor 1973-1974 Nell Clare 1975-1976 Elsie Webb 1977 Vera Bennett 1978 M Sheppard 1979-1980-1981 Verna Bennett 1982 Cory Butenhuis 1983 Marge Sheppard 1984 Ruth Ford 1985 Olive Buchanan 1986 Gladys Morton 1987 Ev Scanlon 1988 Olive Buchanan 1989 Marguerite Bowness 1990 Alice Wagstaff 1991 Mary Varney 1992-1993 Sheilagh Larsen 1994

Cathie Chambers 1995 Joy Boyes 1996 Ethel Simpson 1997 Bev Reber 1998 Evelyn Scanlan 1999-2000 Lois Kaye 2002 Joyce Hope 2003 Ann Panton 2004 Pat Chern 2005 Joyce Hope 2006 Helen Williams 2007 Joan Williams 2008 Maureen Adams 2009 Shirley McGill

Qualicum Beach Memorial Golf Club Ladies Captain's Trophy – Eclectic Low Gross: 1977 Joy Boyes 1978 Happy Boughen 1979-1980 Joy Boyes 1981 Happy Boughen 1982 Audrey Koke & Joy Boyes 1983 Audrey Koke 1984-1985 Joy Boyes 1986 Margaret Thompson 1987 Bev Lasure 1988 Colleen Coleman 1989 Margaret Thompson 1990-1991 Daureen Evans 1992 Margaret Thompson 1993 Daureen Evans 1994 Margaret Thompson 1995 Margaret Thompson & Helen Williams 1996 Helen Williams 1997 Bev Lasure 1998-1999 Margaret Thompson 2000 Mikey Aylesworth & Lois Kaye 2001-2002-2003 Lois Kaye 2004 Mikey Aylesworth & Lois Kaye 2005 Edie Gross 2006 Angie Goodman 2007 Sandi Reed 2008 Angie Goodman 2009 Susan Paterson & Angie Goodman 2010 Edie Gross 2011 Maureen Adams & Sara Smith

Qualicum Beach Memorial Golf Club – Men's Captains: 1981 Roland Wickett & Frank Harris 1982 Frank Harris 1983 Jack Parker 1984 Ray Zoost 1985 Wilf Mitchell 1986 Joe Kerr 1987 Gordon Campbell 1988 George Morgan 1989 Ray Morris 1990 Jack Parker 1991 Ted Powell 1992 Ralph Baddeley 1993 Claud Buchanan 1994 Claud Buchanan 1995-1996 Hugh MacNaughton 1997-1998 Gus Barrett 1999-2000 Roy Finck 2001-2002 Terry L'Ami 2003-2004 Ken Vail 2005 George Perry 2006 Larry Windover 2007 Burke Bullock & Bob Smillie 2008 Bob Smillie 2009 John D'Aigle 2010 Bob Smillie & Walter Teichgrab 2011 Bob Benning

Qualicum Beach Memorial Golf Club – Ladies 18 Hole Captains: 1957 Ruby Crowley 1958 Jeannette Forrester 1959 Gladys Darkis 1960 Lockie Montgomery 1961 Anne Parker 1962 Pat Houston 1963 Mary Bullock & Rita Higgs 1964 Ruby Crowley 1965 Jeannette Forrester 1966 Rita Higgs 1967 – 1968 Pat Houston 1970 Rita Higgs 1971-1972 Frances Wilson 1973 Val Monro 1974-1975 Eve Johnson 1976 Thelma Macready 1977-1978 Elsie Webb 1979-1980 Bev Lasure 1981 Joy Boyes 1982-1983 Verna Bennett 1985-1986 Nel Clare 1987 Mary Bullock 1988 Colleen Coleman 1990-1991 Blanche Barrett 1992 Beth McKinnon 1993-1994 Joan Jeffs 1995-1996 Helen Williams 1997-1998 Mary Moore 1999-2000 Doreen Lawter 2001-2002 Ruth Brodie 2003-2004 Maureen Adams 2005-2006 Lynn Buchanan 2007-2008 Sandi Reed 2009-2010 Lynn Backus 2011 Sandi Reed

Qualicum Beach Memorial Golf Club Ladies 9 Hole Captains: 1991 Ev Swinburne 1992 Marilyn Erickson 1993 Tibby Davis 1994 Jane MacDonald 1995 Betty Blackie 1996 Martha Sundquist 1997 Joy Sutherland 1998 Win Trusdale 1999 Bernice Sloper 2000 Jean Crawshaw 2001 Marg Deering 2002 Pat Rooke 2003 Meta van Pelt 2004 June Dunn 2005 Jean Spec 2006 Bernice Sloper 2007 Elaine Mooney 2008 Elaine Mooney 2009 Shirley Layman 2010 Marg De Hart 2011 Pat Rooke